PRAISE FOR
The Power of Visual Storytelling

"Smart marketers know that visual storytelling is the essential new skill in everything marketing and social. This book is not only a complete overview of the breakout trend but, most importantly, the key to doing it right, a total Right Hook!"

—**GARY VAYNERCHUK,** *New York Times* bestselling author of *Crush It!* and *Jab, Jab, Jab, Right Hook*

"A valuable guide to understanding how to develop powerful marketing programs using the art of visual storytelling."

—**GUY KAWASAKI,** author of *APE: Author, Publisher, Entrepreneur* and former chief evangelist of Apple

"*The Power of Visual Storytelling* is the new marketing bible! Filled with proven examples and practical how-tos, this book is the road map to engaging customers like never before."

—**NANCY BHAGAT,** Vice President, Global Marketing Strategy and Campaigns, Intel

"Social media trailblazers Walter and Gioglio take us on a ride into the hottest new marketing trend, visual storytelling. A must-read for the C-suite, savvy marketers, and anyone looking to succeed in the social era."

—**JEFFREY HAYZLETT,** primetime television host of Bloomberg TV and bestselling author

"If a picture is worth a thousand words, *The Power of Visual Storytelling* is worth a million."

—**SCOTT MONTY,** Manager, Global Digital and Multimedia Communications, Ford Motor Company

"Ekaterina and Jessica not only live visual marketing, they help define it. If you're in marketing or in any form of customer engagement, this book is for you."

—**BRIAN SOLIS,** visual storyteller and author of *What's the Future of Business: Changing the Way Businesses Create Experiences*

"A visually stunning, intelligent, and practical book, *The Power of Visual Storytelling* is the guidebook for innovative marketing in the digital era. This book has it all!"

—**CHIP CONLEY,** founder of Joie de Vivre Hospitality and author of *Peak*

"Learn from experts Walter and Gioglio how to harness the emotional power of pictures. Tapping years of hands-on experience, the authors marry a deep knowledge of tools and best practices with a framework to create a coherent strategy road map. You'll want to keep this book close by as you engage on the social web!"

—**CHARLENE LI,** *New York Times* bestselling author of *Open Leadership* and founder of Altimeter Group

"Ekaterina Walter and Jessica Gioglio are insightful, horizon thinkers who have an incredible ability to identify emerging trends, technologies, and platforms and then translate them into practical application, which makes *The Power of Storytelling* an invaluable combination of strategic know-how and tactical how-to."

> **—CHRISTINE CEA,** Senior Director, Marketing Communications, Unilever

"Walter and Gioglio have nailed it. With everything from 'why' to 'how,' this new book will quickly become a marketer's new best friend! Visual storytelling has unimaginable potential for businesses, and this book offers the tips, tools, and advice for putting it to use."

> **—ROD BROOKS,** CMO, PEMCO Insurance

"A visual representation is much easier to understand (and remember) than pages of text or columns of numbers. Ekaterina and Jessica show the art and science of visual storytelling and how to make these critical components part of any successful new marketing plan."

> **—DAVID MEERMAN SCOTT,** bestselling author of *The New Rules of Marketing & PR*

"This book is timely, provocative, beautiful, more than a little frightening, and 100 percent required reading for all marketers. Online business success is largely driven by pictures, not words. This is the playbook for visual marketing in today's 'right now' world. Highly recommended."

> **—JAY BAER,** *New York Times* bestselling author of *Youtility*

"Visual storytelling is essential in today's crowded world, and this book is a vital read to understand it. I give it two giant orange thumbs up!"

> **—DAVE KERPEN,** *New York Times* bestselling author of *Likeable Social Media* and *Likeable Leadership*

"Brands are missing the point when it comes to marketing in this day and age . . . and that's the entire point of this great book. The best brands are using text, images, audio, and video to tell their own, unique stories. *The Power of Visual Storytelling* is the perfect place for your brand to get started."

> **—MITCH JOEL,** President, Twist Image, and author of *CTRL ALT Delete* and *Six Pixels of Separation*

"*The Power of Visual Storytelling* is invaluable for all marketers as brands become their own content creators, and even, dare I say, publishers. I recommend it to any media, brand, and marketing strategist. It's certainly required reading for my marketing team."

> **—CHRISTINE OSEKOSKI,** Publisher, *Fast Company*

"This book is 'picture perfect' for brand-builders looking to exploit the full and increasingly important power of visual storytelling."

> **—PETE BLACKSHAW,** Global Head of Design & Social Media, Nestlé, and author of *Satisfied Customers Tell Three Friends, Angry Customers Tell 3000*

THE POWER OF
VISUAL
STORYTELLING

THE POWER OF VISUAL STORYTELLING

How to Use Visuals, Videos, and Social Media to Market Your Brand

EKATERINA WALTER
JESSICA GIOGLIO

New York   Chicago   San Francisco   Athens   London   Madrid
Mexico City   Milan   New Delhi   Singapore   Sydney   Toronto

1 2 3 4 5 6 7 8 9 0   DOW/DOW   1 9 8 7 6 5 4

ISBN   978-0-07-182393-7
MHID   0-07-182393-X

e-ISBN 978-0-07-182400-2
e-MHID   0-07-182400-6

Library of Congress Cataloging-in-Publicaton Data

Walter, Ekaterina
     The power of visual storytelling : how to use visuals, videos, and social media to market your brand / by Ekaterina Walter and Jessica Gioglio. — 1 Edition.
        pages cm
        ISBN-13: 978-0-07-182393-7 (alk. paper)
        ISBN-10: 0-07-182393-X (alk. paper)
     1. Viral marketing. 2. Internet marketing. I. Gioglio, Jessica. II. Title.
     HF5415.1265.W365 2014
     659.14'4—dc23
                                                                                    2013041728

McGraw-Hill Education books are available at special quantity discounts to use as premiums and sales promotions or for use in corporate training programs. To contact a representative, please visit the Contact Us pages at www.mhprofessional.com.

To all of the marketers who are embracing the
art of visual storytelling and who see every day
as an opportunity for adventure and innovation.
You have redefined how we facilitate meaningful
relationships with our customers, and you inspire us
to push the limits of what's possible every day.

Contents

Foreword

Writing has a dirty little secret. Authors don't admit it, editors deny it, and publishers repress it. This secret is so explosive that if ever exposed, it would bring the literary world to its knees. Or so the literary world believes. Want to know what the secret is? Pictures.

For 32,000 years, people have drawn. We've written for only 5,000. (And since the first written languages were pictorial, even that date is debatable.)

Let me share a few data points:

1. J.K. Rowling, the most successful author of our generation, finally admitted two years ago that she drew Harry Potter's world before she wrote it.
2. J.R.R. Tolkien drew Middle Earth before writing of it. *The Lord of the Rings* was originally intended to be illustrated, but his publisher said no. (His books of drawings became available only after the success of Peter Jackson's movies.)
3. Before he wrote *On the Road*, Jack Kerouac drew a mandala to visualize his plotlines.

4 Joseph Heller created a visual timeline to help keep track of the action in *Catch 22*.

5 Vladimir Nabokov had to create a map of James Joyce's *Ulysses* in order to follow the narrative.

The list goes on. As students of literature and imagination, did we ever know this?

We did not. Strange, isn't it? Pictures are the basis of our storytelling, but no one seems to want to admit it.

Our verbal mind does not work without our visual mind. Those of us raised in the western educational tradition find that terrifying. Pictures trivialize, drawings are silly, doodles patronize, art is decoration. These are the things we're told in school.

In this marvelous book, Ekaterina Walter and Jessica Gioglio show us how wrong we are.

Thinking in pictures is our nature. Sharing those pictures has long been our dream. With the arrival of global social media, we have a whole new set of tools to make that dream come true.

Thank you, Ekaterina and Jessica, for showing us those tools. This is going to be fun.

DAN ROAM
San Francisco, 2013

Introduction

I t was "one of those days." Nothing was going as planned, and stress was mounting. Ekaterina sat back in her chair. She knew everything would work out, but that didn't make the day less frustrating. A minute later she knew what she needed. It was time for . . . a boost. As any self-respecting social media strategist would do, she turned to Twitter, typed "It's been one of those days today . . . @benefitbeauty #beautyboost," and hit tweet. Thirty seconds later a tweet came back from Benefit Cosmetics. The tweet contained a pink-and-white image that said, "If being sexy was a crime, you'd be guilty as charged." Ekaterina couldn't help but smile. All it took was just one little tweet, she thought. The tweet was immediately shared. It was discussed in the office. It made women (and men, for that matter) smile. It was a hit. At that moment everyone's day felt just a little bit brighter.

Instantly transported away from their tough day, several people found themselves inspired by how the use of visual content in real time gave them a different perspective and, indirectly, admiration for a brand.

As marketers, we appreciate the way #BeautyBoost visuals tell an ongoing story of how Benefit Cosmetics wants its consumers to feel good about themselves. The company even touts in its Twitter bio, "Laughter is the

It's been one of those days today...
@benefitbeauty #beautyboost

If being sexy was a crime, you'd be guilty as charged.

By Benefit Cosmetics @BenefitBeauty

"I've learned that people will forget what you said, people will forget what you did, but people will never forget how you made them feel."[1]

—MAYA ANGELOU

best cosmetic . . . so grin and wear it!" The compliments are sent individually to members of Benefit's online community, and they are humorously written with a wink and a smile, without being overly promotional. With beauty pick-up themed one-liners like, "Your lashes are longer than a supermodel's legs," or, "Your skin is so radiant, satellites in orbit can see your glow," the compliments nod to Benefit's being a beauty brand, without putting specific products in the spotlight.

Claudia Allwood, director of U.S. digital marketing for Benefit Cosmetics, says:

> We wanted to create visual, shareable content that conveyed our brand's central message: laughter is the best cosmetic. We wanted something as instant as our beauty solutions, as clever as our brand's personality, and as social as our consumers. Benefit is not about unachievable beauty; our products are your best friend that comes through in a flash to bring out your natural beauty in five minutes. With our #BeautyBoost campaign we wanted to surprise women and delight them with instant affirmations that they are gorgeous just the way they are.

Sure, Benefit could have simply tweeted an uplifting one-liner via text, but the gesture of incorporating a visual was far more powerful for several reasons. First and foremost, it made its recipients pause their busy day and appreciate the intended message. Next, it prompted the recipients to share the image with their community of friends and followers (not to mention sharing the story in this book!), encouraging positive word of mouth for the

You turn us on more than a light switch.

benefit

If "irresistible" isn't your middle name, it should be.

benefit

Your complexion is smoother than a pick-up artist.

benefit

Your skin is so radiant, satellites in orbit can see your glow.

benefit

Your lashes are longer than a supermodel's legs.

benefit

Your hair is shinier than pirate treasure.

benefit

You're hotter than a curling iron.

benefit

If you were words on a page, you'd be 'fine print.'

benefit

Benefit brand. Last, the interaction and content were memorable, prompting an increase in perception, loyalty, and respect for the company.

This is precisely why we wrote this book on the power of visual storytelling. Visual storytelling, when done correctly, has the potential to enhance loyalty, strengthen customer relationships, increase awareness, and more. Social media communities and blogs have redefined how we connect with one another, search for information, and build relationships online. The challenge and opportunity for marketers is to embrace the new rules of engagement and think creatively about how the use of visuals can support their goals. Research proves that there's a scientific reason why people respond to visuals more strongly and quickly than text alone, but content for content's sake just won't move the needle anymore. Companies and brands need to strive for more by embracing the art of visual storytelling. Understanding who you are as a brand, what you stand for, and what goals you're trying to achieve in tandem with what your customers are looking for from your company can be crafted into a powerful, creative visual story.

> In the age of infobesity, there are several ways to stand out from the noise and draw attention to your content in an organic way. And visual storytelling is one of them.

It's almost ironic to be writing a book when the visual storytelling leaders we see today leverage very little text in favor of images, videos, and other illustrations on their social media channels. This is why you'll notice that we paid careful attention to the layout, size, and use of images in this book. We understand that in order to educate and inspire our readers, text is needed, but we also feel that supplementing case studies and examples with compelling visuals will strengthen our key points and takeaways.

We took this approach to personify the continued, powerful shift to welcome visual storytelling. Just look at how far Facebook has come—where text once reigned supreme, the News Feed has transformed into a never-ending visual magazine filled with relevant information about the people and companies you care about the most. Sites like Twitter have evolved from text only to integrating a mobile-friendly experience where images and videos shine. YouTube is so popular that it's now ranked the number two search engine after Google. SlideShare has made the PowerPoint presentation cool again. Numbers geeks are now celebrated for their brilliant data communicated through clever infographics. And don't even get us started on how much creativity there is to be had across relative "newcomers" Pinterest, Instagram, and Vine.

Pause for a moment and truly take in just how much social media have evolved over the past few years. The proliferation of social media platforms is fun, exciting, and also a bit daunting. Companies can easily drive themselves crazy trying to be all things to all people across so many platforms and hours of the day.

The purpose of this book isn't to make you feel like your company needs to be doing everything under the sun. Instead, we're here to share why visual storytelling is valuable and easy to adopt, even if you don't have a massive staff or budget. Our goal in writing this book is to share a mix of our personal experiences and insider tips gleaned from working for celebrated, industry-leading companies that embraced the art of visual storytelling early on. We've been in the trenches producing content from scratch, and we have learned firsthand how to craft visuals into a compelling story. We've seen successes, dealt with misses, and even managed a few crises in the process.

As a result, it was important to focus on news and takeaways you can actually use. Some of these are big-picture strategies, and some are "in-the-weeds" tactics that will help inform and enhance your day-to-day content calendar planning. We've included the types of visual media at your disposal and platform-specific best practices, as well as powerful case studies on how other companies use visual storytelling to stand out on their social media channels. Throughout the book, we've sprinkled in a range of case studies across B2B and B2C industries. We believe that some of the best ideas can be inspired by others and reworked into a unique concept that's relevant to your company.

Working as social media strategists and evangelists for brands such as Dunkin' Donuts and Intel, we wanted to share our knowledge, experiences, and overall journey of social business innovation. But in the end, we

Visual storytelling isn't just a shiny new phenomenon. It's here to stay, and it will continue to evolve as new social media platforms enter into the mix. As this happens, leveraging photos, videos, infographics, presentations, and more will only increase in importance.

wrote this book because we're not just social media enthusiasts. We're also consumers. We know that consumers are faced with more messages and social media platforms than ever before, resulting in shrinking consumer attention spans. Making an impact and breaking through the clutter is harder than ever before, so it's important to focus your time, energy, and resources on the right strategies and tactics.

There is no time like the present to get started and begin creating!

CHAPTER 1

The Rise of Visual Storytelling

W e've all heard marketers proclaim that "content is king," but the rise of visual social media platforms like Pinterest and Instagram coupled with Facebook's multimillion-dollar acquisition of the latter have ushered in an era in which the old adage "a picture is worth a thousand words" is more relevant than ever. Today marketers are turning to visuals to amplify social media engagement—and for good reason.

But simply posting images, videos, and other visuals isn't enough. Companies that go beyond creating and sharing content to embrace visual storytelling are emerging as the leaders of the pack and are being rewarded with engagement, referral traffic, and even sales. The rise of visual social media platforms has also resulted in the "Now! Economy," in which consumers welcome real-time

> Marketing is creating products and services that lead your tribe to tell stories that spread.
>
> **—SETH GODIN,** bestselling author of *All Marketers Are Liars: The Power of Telling Authentic Stories in a Low Trust World*

Posts that include an album or picture receive 120 to 180% more engagement from fans than text-based posts.[1] On Instagram, users post 40 million photos per day with upward of 8,500 likes and 1,000 comments per second.[2] There are an astounding 3 billion views on YouTube daily.[3]

Visual storytelling is defined as the use of images, videos, infographics, presentations, and other visuals on social media platforms to craft a graphical story around key brand values and offerings.

marketing in the form of snackable bits of visual content. From creating Pinterest boards to make meal planning easier to sharing images and videos that will brighten someone's day, consumers are gobbling up visual content as it's relevant to them.

Instead of relying on text-heavy content, a successful visual storytelling strategy requires a "show, don't tell," approach with the goal of generating more potential for engagement, conversation, and sharing.

In a time when social media and blogs are estimated to reach 80% of all active U.S. Internet users, engagement and action have become the new gold standard.[4] Whether it's using Pinterest to find favors for a baby shower or watching a YouTube case study that encourages a meeting with a new service provider, visual storytelling is helping companies to break through the clutter and propel action as never before.

Take Sephora, for example. The company has noted that its Pinterest followers spend 15 times more than its Facebook fans.[5] The company has more than 200,000 followers on Pinterest, with boards such as "Travel," "Nailspotting," "Beauty How-Tos," and others. Sephora also has a board containing its "Most Popular Pins," which shares the pins that are generating hundreds of repins and likes.

Or the Calgary Zoo, which generated national headlines and interest in its annual report by swapping a traditional PDF for an Instagram. Proclaiming its 2012 annual report "The Year of the Penguins," 55 photos and captions served as the report pages and content, telling the story of what the zoo had accomplished over the course of the year in a unique, highly visual way.

And who hasn't heard of the visual storytelling revolution that Blendtec generated after launching the viral "Will It Blend?" series? Inspired by an R&D video that blended wooden boards together, the company's marketing team decided to invest $100 in other wacky supplies and began sharing videos on its YouTube channel with the simple question "Will it blend?" One of the favorites among the consumers was the video that blended the latest iPhone into tiny pieces.

The Evolution of Visual Storytelling

Visual storytelling has not been an overnight sensation, but instead it has been the result of a continued evolution of social media platforms, along with user and company behaviors. From the late 1990s to mid-2000s, sites such as blogging platforms, Myspace, Delicious (formerly Del.icio.us), Flickr, and Facebook created early opportunities for visual engagement. If you look closely at these platforms, you'll see that all of them were created in response to the massive flow of content on the Internet, much of which was visual. Even back then, blog entries with visuals performed better than those without. Myspace offered users multiple opportunities to personalize their user profiles, from the background to the music and content shared. Flickr rose in popularity as an early photo sharing site, and today it still houses a passionate community of photo enthusiasts, plus professional and hobbyist photographers.

Besides the content shared, perhaps one of the most important qualities these early social media platform leaders had was the ability to bring like-minded individuals together online. Just as today, when there are so many social media platforms to engage

on, like-minded individuals always seemed to find their way into the online communities that best reflected their interests. The key then, as it is now, was to identify what brings people to a social media platform, understand what value they derive from the platform, and determine how your company could fit within those engagement best practices.

In addition to community engagement, the activity on these platforms also reinforced that users were looking for ways to easily share and organize content, imagery, visuals, and videos. From following your favorite bloggers on LiveJournal, to curating a branded profile on Myspace complete with your favorite songs and music videos, or building photo albums on Flickr, it's no surprise that the saying "Content Is King" was born—and subsequently overused for years to come. Content has always been the hook for inspiring action or engagement across social media channels, but the rules have changed as platforms have continued to evolve.

The evolution of Facebook's layout from 2004 to 2013 offers a unique look at the continued changes social media platforms are taking to pave the way for visual content and storytelling. Facebook has evolved from a text-heavy format favoring user profiles and group pages to a vibrant News Feed filled with colorful photos, videos, and more. With newcomers like Pinterest, Instagram, and Vine, it's clear that Facebook users also crave clean layouts and the ability to quickly scroll through content in order to find what they're looking for. The rise of mobile users on Facebook also indicates that users want a seamless experience regardless of the device they're viewing the site on.

When Facebook first launched in 2004, it was simply a directory of user names, interests, and contact information. You had to navigate to a user's profile to learn more about that person or to leave a comment on his or her Wall. The layout was text heavy, and the most prominent image was a user's profile photo. Joining groups and sharing your interests on your profile helped Facebook users to foster engagement and cultivate an identity for themselves on the site.

Facebook took first steps toward a more visual experience on September 5, 2006, with the News Feed and the Mini-Feed. The News Feed was visible on your Facebook home page, and it offered a personalized collection of information curated by your activities, groups you belonged to, photos your friends were tagged in, and more. The Mini-Feed offered updates on what had been changed to a user's Facebook profile.[6] Rather quickly users began to see the value in reading their friends' status updates and seeing photos as part of a stream of news. The experience ultimately paved the way for today's Facebook News Feed layout.

The continued shift toward a more visual Facebook user experience continued from 2007 to 2012. From tabs, to apps, groups, and pages, users began to "like" the pages created by companies and public figures as a way to showcase their interest in them. In 2007, Facebook was filtering an average of 30,000 News Feed story updates into a customized stream of 60 stories for each user every day.[7] As a result, securing a text placement in the News Feed was equated to getting into the first page of Google's search results.[8] However, brands couldn't secure this premium placement without paying, developing an app, or inserting an ad next to News Feed items.[9] In 2008, apps boomed in popularity, and status updates emerged as a tool that companies could use to share valuable content and images within their pages or groups. But this content was mostly distributed either through an inbox message or an update notification to view the post.[10] Users could then decide if they cared to learn more and visit the page, app, or group, requiring the content to work that much harder.

In 2011, the launch of Facebook Timeline completely shook up the Facebook user experience—in a good way. Promising you an opportunity to "tell your life story with a new kind of profile," images, videos, and interactive content rose in prominence over Facebook's previous text-heavy environment. Users now had the opportunity to craft a highly interactive, sharable, digital, scrapbooklike layout with a cover photo, they could use large images, and they could organize important historical information about themselves. Featuring a similar experience for brands, Timeline for brands allowed brand pages to promote visual content in a completely new way, with the results to prove it. In 2012, just one month

after the introduction of Facebook Timeline for brands, visual content—photos and videos—saw a 65% increase in engagement.[11]

In 2013, Facebook announced its first major update to its News Feed since the launch of Timeline in 2011. At the press conference to introduce the News Feed redesign, Mark Zuckerberg said, "How we're all sharing is changing, and the News Feed needs to evolve with those changes. This is the evolving face of News Feed."[12] The changes introduced a stronger focus on images, mobile optimization, and access to multiple feeds. Of the more than 1 billion monthly active users that existed as of December 2012, 543 million monthly active users were now using Facebook's mobile products.[13] According to Facebook, shifting user behavior also showcased that 50% of status updates now included an image, and posts with images far outperformed those with just text alone.[14]

Compared to the earlier years when companies curated experiences around highly branded pages, apps, and groups, the new rules of Facebook engagement dictate that the majority of interactions happen in the News Feed. Users now visit Facebook to catch up with what their friends are up to, seek out specific information, or share content, such as vacation photos. This behavior is consistent across many social media platforms, except for Pinterest, which is more focused on the sharing and categorizing of visual content.

While challenging for brands to hear, the reality is that users in most cases are not going on social media sites like Facebook to view brand-generated content. Meaning, brands now must strive to be a welcome interruption inside the News Feed. Visual content must be attention-grabbing and prompt action or affinity in order to remain relevant, or it risks being "unliked." On Facebook, users can also hide anyone in their network, including companies, from their News Feed, which is worse than an unlike, as brands cannot measure how many people still like them but have hidden their status updates from their News Feeds.

These changes, coupled with the introduction of EdgeRank, an algorithm introduced by Facebook to determine where and which posts will appear on a user's News Feed, have placed a greater value on visual engagement and storytelling within the digital news stream.

With more engagement on Facebook taking place in the News Feed than ever, quality images and videos stand out more than text status updates, and they generate more engagement. The more frequently users reward company posts with positive engagement, the better chance those posts have of making it into their fans' News Feeds. Engagement and sharing from those fans will help to reach new audiences through the "friend-of-friend" effect, prompting fan growth and increased engagement.

As a result of EdgeRank, companies cannot rest on their laurels. Each piece of content must be generated with affinity, weight, and timing in mind. How often someone engages with a brand's content, coupled with the volume and sentiment of those interactions, helps dictate what Facebook users deem interesting.

Over the past several years Facebook has been criticized for the introduction of an algorithm that decides what people see or not see. Marketers have been complaining that they work hard to grow their Facebook fans to large numbers, only to have the algorithm "choose" whom to serve the relevant content to, thus allowing only small numbers of fans from the overall fan base to see every single update that brands post.

The reality is that in the age of infobesity, social networks, search engines, and mobile applications will incorporate more and more filtering tools to ensure that the content that is served up to consumers is relevant to them. And the role of marketers is, and always has been (whether it is in mass media or digital media), to produce the best, most relevant content to break through the filtering algorithms and into the consumers' digital news streams.

The History and the Rise of Visual Storytelling

Fast forward to the present, and there's a proliferation of social media platforms as never before—with impressive audience sizes to match. From Facebook to Twitter, Instagram, Pinterest, Tumblr, YouTube, SlideShare, and Vine, each platform offers unique opportunities for visual storytelling and engagement. The wealth of social media platforms relates back to user behavior and how consumers prefer to receive information and connect online. Mobile use has skyrocketed globally, with 6.8 billion mobile subscriptions at the end of 2012, which is equivalent to 96% of the world population.[15] With cameras in the vast majority of people's pockets, it's no surprise that platforms such as Instagram and Vine have been specifically designed for mobile audiences and then subsequently acquired by social media such as Facebook and Twitter.

Similar to past adoption patterns of social media platforms, people are continuously looking for tools, resources, and communities that will make their busy lives easier. Facebook has always been the grand dame for keeping tabs on friends and family, but the rise of platforms like Twitter, Pinterest, and SlideShare has been fueled by people's desires for solutions that add value. It's why people turn to Twitter for real-time information when a breaking news event happens or to Pinterest for interior design tips and meal planning. SlideShare is now a go-to resource for business information and education.

Another contributor to the rise in visual storytelling is the on-the-go nature of people's lives and their interest in sharing user-generated imagery and visuals in real time. With smartphones always within an arm's reach for many consumers, the ability to snap a photo or record a video and share it on social media channels has never been easier. It's why social media platforms like Facebook, Twitter, Instagram, Tumblr, YouTube, and Vine continue to boom in popularity—they facilitate ease and convenience of sharing in the moment.

So why is the sharing of visuals and videos so important to both consumers and companies? Delving deeper into research around user behavior on popular web and social media sites reveals that the proof is in the visual pudding.

Research indicates that consumer interest in visual content isn't necessarily just a preference; it's actually easier and faster for humans to process. The right picture can go further than just telling your story visually; it can make you feel emotions, evoke memories, and even make you act differently.

Humans are wired to process visuals differently than text and to respond differently to pictures than to words. Although human communication has existed for about 30,000 years, it has been only in the last 7,000 years that humans developed a written language.[16] Although our wonderful brains translate marks and squiggles into words, it doesn't come as naturally to the mind as processing images.

Let me show you what I mean.

Read this word:

GIRL

What does it make you think of? Do you have a specific girl in mind? What age is she? What is she doing? Does that word itself evoke any emotions?

Now look at this image:

What does it make you think? What does it make you *feel*?

Images don't just paint a thousand words. They can communicate some things far more specific than words—specific emotions, specific feelings,

Visuals are processed 60,000 times faster than text by the human brain and 90% of information transmitted to the brain is visual.[17] Humans evolved over millennia to respond to visual information long before they developed the ability to read text.

specific moods, things that are almost impossible to convey using words. Do you think that if 100 people heard the word "girl," they would all think of the same thing, exactly? Would they all *feel* the same thing? But looking at a picture like the one on the previous page, the majority of people will think and feel something very similar.

Images act like shortcuts to the brain: we are visual creatures, and we are programmed to react to visuals more than to words. In the 1960s, Professor Albert Mehrabian showed that 93% of communication is in fact nonverbal.[18] By this he meant that most of the feelings and attitudes of a message come from the facial expressions and the way the words are said, and the rest, only 7%, derives from the actual words being spoken. It isn't even just the meanings of a message that are conveyed more precisely by visual information. Even issues of trust and credibility are carried by images far more so than text.

Dan Roam, an expert on visual storytelling and an author of the international bestseller *The Back of the Napkin: Solving Problems and Selling Ideas with Pictures*, says:

> We live in a world that is very noisy. There are a lot of conversations and buzzwords around us. The number one way out of this noise is just to become visual. To show things with pictures. For thousands of years people have been drawing. If you think about the history of communication from then till now, it goes through all the different periods of time where people are trying to find ways to share information with each other. For the longest time, it was through telling stories around the campfire, reciting poems, and singing songs. That was the technology that was available. All along, all we wanted to do was share pictures with each other. Painting was the only way to convey a message visually. Then came writing and the printing press. Now let's

jump forward to today. Holy smokes, what do we have available? It's like mankind's greatest dream is available at our fingertips. I want to share a story with you, and I want to share it with you visually: all I have to do is take a picture and e-mail it to you. I put it on Twitter, or I post it on Facebook, Flickr, or Instagram. It's no surprise that we are sharing billions of images on those networks. It makes perfect sense—we've always wanted to share pictures with each other, but we never had the right technology to do it. Now we do. That, to me, is the biggest trend in marketing and communication, period. The "simple" technologies that we now have are enabling us to do what we have always dreamed of doing, which was to easily share ideas with each other in pictorial form.

STATS

Research from Billion Dollar Graphics has shown that 46.1% of people say a website's design is the number one criterion for discerning the credibility of the company,[19] while MDG Advertising has demonstrated that 67% of consumers consider clear, detailed images to be very important and carry even more weight than the product information, full description, and customer ratings.[20]

We can't get away from the importance of visuals in our everyday communication. That much is clear. But what does this mean to marketers?

Creating images that make the viewer think and feel a certain way is big business to advertising: getting the right visuals is at the very heart of business branding. In 2001, Pepsi budgeted over $1 billion on its image. Not to be outdone, Coca-Cola budgeted $1.4 billion for its image in the same year.[21]

Empathizing in the intended way to symbols and images is reliant on a shared cultural identity—that is, on an understanding of who your audience is. Different cultures, and even different demographics, will process symbols differently. Whereas images such as star-spangled flags and eagles can appeal to an American sense of patriotism, the same effect may be achieved by a maple leaf, a lion, or a kangaroo in other countries. And what appears strong and decisive to one audience could seem aggressive to another.

Brian Solis, an author of *What's the Future of Business*, says: "The most effective visual storytelling affects one's being . . . changing perspective and ultimately behavior upon impact."

Creating the right image to convey your message relies on understanding whom you are communicating with and how they will react to it. Communication is a two-way process, and marketers have to be as sure of their audience as they are of the images they are crafting to reach them. The right graphics can persuade, relate, and influence decisions on an emotional and subconscious level. Images are powerful tools, and we are becoming an ever-more visual culture.

This data is precisely why visual storytelling allows companies a strong opportunity to take these existing behaviors and cultivate content focused on harnessing consumer engagement versus broadcasting messages. Visuals draw immediate attention to a post about a topic and can generate shares, traffic, lead generation, thought leadership, and expertise. Visual storytelling can also help companies achieve earned media at scale. By striving to be shareworthy with all visual content, companies like Coca-Cola are reaching the valued friends-of-friends audience. This allows Coca-Cola to better leverage word-of-mouth endorsements, which are incredibly valuable. According to Bazaar Voice, 51% of Americans trust user-generated content over other information on a company website.[22]

> Graphics are used as a shortcut to an idea that causes the audience to respond in a certain way. An image becomes a symbol of something bigger and more complex: this is what lies behind the psychology of logos and advertising imagery.

For B2C companies, this sentiment is especially prevalent in the fashion industry where there's a trend of trusting the opinions of bloggers and customer reviews. Why? People like seeing how the garments are styled and fit by people they can relate to.

In spring 2013, Coach launched a campaign asking its customers to admire the view from above—of their shoes! Using the #coachfromabove hashtag, fans were asked to share "selfie" photos of their Coach shoes on Instagram or Twitter for a chance to be featured in a gallery on the company's website. A "selfie" is a photo you take of yourself. Over an eight-week timeframe, Coach's user-generated campaign secured an average of 80 images per week and stretched the content across its website, a Facebook album, Pinterest board, live events, and blogger and influencer outreach. The end result was a continuous stream of highly editorial images similar to what you might see on a fashion blog or in a magazine.

Not to be outdone by their B2C counterparts, a reported 91% of B2B companies are now using content marketing tactics to reach their target audiences.[23] With the top social media platforms ranking from LinkedIn, to Twitter, Facebook, and YouTube, B2B companies are also embracing visual content to enhance their content marketing strategies. From assisting with lead generation and customer retention, to augmenting expertise and industry leadership, the value of visually relevant content is rising in importance.

HubSpot is a fantastic example of a B2B company that leverages visual content and storytelling across a number of social media channels. While many of the company's social media channels are impressive, HubSpot's Pinterest presence showcases how B2B companies can let their personality and creativity shine in a way that encourages engagement with influencers and prospective clients. With boards dedicated to company culture, helpful e-books, webinars, and infographics, the visual content shared is a mix of informative, humorous and

inspiring. If you've ever thought that B2B companies should only be serious, think again. Hysterical boards like "Meme-tastic Marketing" and "Awful Stock Photography" show other businesses that it's okay to have a little fun. As a result of their efforts, HubSpot has more than 17,000 followers on Pinterest, and it can leverage the channel to create inbound links and to drive traffic, search engine optimization (SEO), and engagement.

These are just some of the examples of brands' using visual storytelling to engage with their customers. Now let's look at the types, tips, and tactics of visual marketing.

Key STATS for Marketers to Consider

- 90% of information transmitted to the brain is visual, and visuals are processed in the brain 60,000 times faster than text.[24]
- 40% of people respond better to visual information than to plain text.[25]
- Studies have shown that the average modern adult attention span is somewhere between 2.8 and 8 seconds.[26]
- The visual networks Tumblr, Pinterest, and Instagram all grew during 2012, dubbed the "the rise of the visual web" by ComScore.[27]
- 94% more total views on average are attracted by content containing compelling images than content without images.[28]
- 67% of consumers consider clear, detailed images to be very important and to carry even more weight than the product information, full description, and customer ratings.[29]
- Posting plenty of visual content is a sure way of boosting engagement: a recent study of 739,000 tweets found that 76% of content that was shared had a photo attached, and 18% had a video as part of the message.[30]
- 62% of respondents to a survey from the Custom Content Council reported using video in their content marketing.[31]
- A 37% increase in engagement is experienced when Facebook posts include photographs.[32]
- A 14% increase in page views is seen when press releases contain a photograph. (Page views climb 48% when both photographs and videos are included.)[33]

Key STATS for Marketers to Consider, *continued*

- 46.1% of people say a website's design is the number one criterion for discerning the credibility of the company.[34]
- Publishers who use infographics grow in traffic an average of 12% more than those who don't.[35]
- Posts with videos attract three times more inbound links than plain text posts attract.[36]
- Viewers spend 100% more time on pages with videos.[37]
- Viewers are 85% more likely to purchase a product after watching a product video.[38]
- Images are becoming ever more central to our lives: of all the photos ever taken by humankind, 10% have been taken in the last 12 months.[39]
- Articles with images get 94% more total views.[40]

- Including a photo and a video in a press release increases views by over 45%.[41]
- 60% of consumers are more likely to consider or contact a business when an image shows up in local search results.[42]
- In an e-commerce site, 67% of consumers say the quality of a product image is "very important" in selecting and purchasing a product.[43]
- In an online store, customers think that the quality of a product's image is more important than product-specific information (63%), a long description (54%), and ratings and reviews (53%).[44]
- A study by EyeViewDigital showed that using video on landing pages can increase conversion by 80%.[45]

Types, Tips, and Tactics of Visual Marketing

From images to videos, infographics, and presentations, the popularity and unprecedented usage of visuals have resulted in a social media era that rewards creativity. A picture may still be worth a thousand words, but memes, quotes, cartoons, and animated GIFs can breathe new life and context into a photo's storytelling capabilities. Even videos, which continue to delight, entertain, and inform, are evolving with consumers' attention spans, whether it's 6 seconds on Vine or 15 seconds on Instagram. Infographics have risen as a valuable tool to communicate stats and the results of research studies. Presentations cater to the vast majority of visual learners and are proven to captivate attention when delving deeper into a given topic.

Types of Visual Content

What follows are some types of visual content that marketers might want to pay attention to.

Images

With the ability to captivate, inspire, motivate, delight, or humor, there are numerous reasons why more than 500 million photos are uploaded and shared every day on average—a number that is projected to double in the next year.[2]

The prevalence of smartphones, coupled with the ease of sharing via social media, has resulted in a culture in which photos are celebrated and in some cases, required. In pop culture, pictures have become so important to consumers that the *Urban Dictionary* now contains the saying "Pics or it didn't happen," meaning that if something really cool or crazy happens to you and it wasn't captured in a photo, your friends may not believe it's true.[3]

In line with consumer photography trends, savvy companies understand that there's more than one way to add a storytelling element on their social media channels through imagery. From traditional images to user-generated content, collages, images with text overlays, memes, and more, there's a lot of creative potential for companies to tap in to. In this section, we'll share image types, photography tips, and examples to help you create well-composed photos that bring different stories and vignettes to life.

Types of Images Used for Visual Storytelling
- Photography
- Graphs and drawings
- User-generated images
- Collages
- Images with text overlays: captions, quotes, and stats
- Word photos
- Memes
- Postcards and e-cards

PHOTOGRAPHY

In many ways, photography is like a blank canvas. Any moment can turn into a photo opportunity, with the beauty in the eye of the photographer.

The photos people take and share across social media platforms showcase how they see and experience their lives, what's important to them, and what they believe is shareworthy with friends and family. For companies looking to amplify their visual storytelling efforts, photographs offer a good starting point.

The concept of well-composed photos is nothing new to companies—it's something they've been sourcing for their websites, advertisements, retail locations, and for the news media for a long time. What's new, though, is the concept of social media–friendly images that drive an immediate response. With professional images, techniques like retouching, food styling, set design, and lighting are commonplace. However, with social media, people are looking for images to be realistic and in line with company values and offerings. By retouching how a model looks in a dress or styling a sandwich to be larger than it really is, you run the risk of generating customer complaints and distrust in your products. Take TripAdvisor, for example, which allows members to post images of their hotel stays. With more than 14 million real images posted to the site, the value of seeing these images is so that consumers can see if the hotel truly matches the images shown on the hotel's website.

GRAPHS AND DRAWINGS

In some cases, when you market a highly technical product, graphs and visualizations may be a better way to go. Some people respond better to charts, graphs, numbers, and visual frameworks. Sometimes putting the concept you are trying to communicate into an easy-to-digest visual framework might make the message you are delivering not only easier to understand but also easier to share with others.

Case in point: when Ekaterina talks about the significance of the word of mouth and brand advocacy with her clients, she talks about the Five Ls of a customer's emotional journey and the fact that the fastest and the most effective way to achieve brand affinity is not through the brand's own messages but through building a strong network of advocates. She points out that the goal of your brand should be to take your *prospective customers* from "Lack of awareness" to "Learning about your brand" to "Like" and to take your *current customers* from "Like" to "Love" to "Loyalty." But it isn't until Ekaterina shows her clients the visual, the framework that explains the Five Ls and brand objectives associated with each one of the stages, that they start smiling and nodding their heads in agreement. It is more powerful when you accompany your message with a visual. Often, no matter how beautiful or impactful your story is, if you include a simple graphic, it'll help your audience establish a deeper understanding and connection with your message.

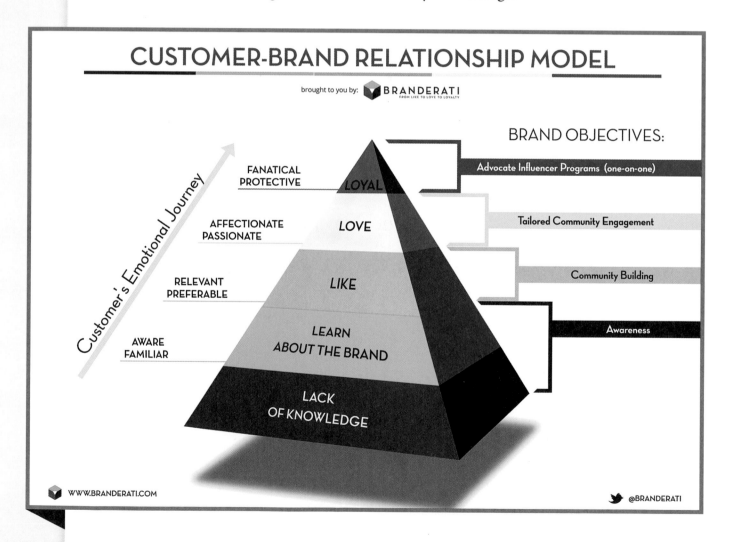

USER-GENERATED IMAGES

Looking to supplement your image library while deepening your relationships with your consumers? Consider developing a program to collect and share user-generated images. By making consumers part of the visual storytelling process, companies are participating in collaborative storytelling while sourcing incredible imagery. Companies get to see firsthand what motivates and inspires their customers, while customers get the validation of seeing their images shared and liked by other fans of the company.

PHOTO COLLAGES

Why use just one image when three, four, or more might tell the story better? Collages are no longer just for scrapbook enthusiasts; they're back in vogue. The concept and motivation are straightforward—you're already snapping and sharing a ton of images, so why not parse them together to help tell a visual story? From highlighting different company or product attributes to weaving in different aspects of an event or curating an inspiration board, collages offer a lot of opportunity for creativity.

IMAGES WITH TEXT OVERLAYS: CAPTIONS, QUOTES, AND STATS

Looking to spice up a traditional image in a way that's easy and cost effective? Want to make sure a photo's caption isn't lost in the social media shuffle? Consider adding a small amount of text. The use of snappy one-liners, quotes, and stats can add a new dimension to your visual storytelling possibilities.

POSTCARDS AND E-CARDS

Social media have not killed the postcard. It has simply reinvented it. Both postcards and e-cards offer a multitude of ways to pair a photo and text together. Whether used in a status update or a Pinterest board, or in a consumer engagement campaign, or in an activation around an event, the nostalgia, convenience, and shareability of an e-card offer companies a unique visual storytelling opportunity.

WORD PHOTOS

From traditional text to quotes and stats, there are many options for using words to enhance the visual story of an image. But what happens if the word is in fact the image? With the help of a few useful tools, like WordFoto, an app for iPhone and iPad Touch, or WordCam Pro for Android, your company's name or tagline, plus key buzzwords, can be turned into an eye-catching visual image.

MEMES

Memes are concepts and ideas that spread from person to person, and they serve as signifiers of the spread of cultural information. In his 1976 book *The Selfish Gene,* Richard Dawkins created the term *meme* from the Greek word "mimeme," which means "an imitated thing."[4] In the 1870s, English photographer Harry Frees started taking photographs of his cats and printing them on the covers of greeting cards, accompanied by humorous text.[5] These cards are the first examples of LOLcats (the most popular and enduring Internet meme—where humorous captions are placed over pictures of cats).

"I can has cheezburger," "Success Kid," "Hipster Ariel," "Bachelor Frog"—these sound like children's superheroes, but they are in fact *memes*—jokes, phrases, concepts, images, videos, and cultural phenomena repeated and shared at an alarming rate. Thanks to the Internet and social media, visual memes can spread globally in a matter of hours. Often nonsensical, usually hilarious, 90% likely to contain an image of a cat, memes are the cultural glue holding the Internet together.

These days, memes appear everywhere, and they spread so fast it is often impossible to discover their source (although you could try www.knowyourmeme.com, which maintains a database on the origins of specific memes).

In the last several years brands have focused on the meme as a tool for awareness and social proof.

Home Depot created its own version of the popular cat meme when it launched "Richard the Cat, a.k.a. Pundit of People," in spring 2013.

Richard gives witty, sarcastic, and snobbish commentary on his human family's DIY adventures. Users can create their own Richard memes, with the chance to win $200 worth of Home Depot vouchers.

Home Depot CMO Trish Mueller credits the origin of the feline meme to an internal meeting last year where she proposed the idea. "Everyone has elves, reindeer, Santa, but one of the biggest things followed in the social space is cats," said Mueller in an interview with *Ad Age*. "When I shared this with our leadership team, our CEO got it immediately."[6] The focus of the Richard campaign is customer engagement by using the meme movement to tell the brand story in a simple and humorous way. With a popular Tumblr blog and a solid Twitter following, Richard is certainly achieving results for the brand.

Cartoons

The artistic, engaging, and humorous nature of cartoons makes this medium a powerful visual storytelling tool. Think back for a moment about your personal experience with cartoons. Many of us grew up with cartoons, from collecting comic books or flipping through the newspaper to uncover the "funnies" section. Cartoons are known for being funny, and viewers delight in uncovering the story and messages through their visual sequence. With so much brand recognition and nostalgia around cartoons, they're inherently eye-catching.

Great messages and ideas for cartoons can come from anywhere, from common customer questions to key products or promotions, pop culture, memes, fun facts, and behind-the-scenes scoops about your company.

Kellogg's Pop-Tarts frequently uses cartoons as part of its visual content mix to tell a fun and irreverent story around people's cravings for Pop-Tarts. Often, the cartoons feature people using sneaky and creative ways to coax their Pop-Tart into a toaster. One such example occurred over the July Fourth holiday, where a cartoon depicted a person luring a Pop-Tart into a toaster made to look like a parade float. While inside the toaster, the Pop-Tart inquires about when to pop out, and the hungry person declares, "Yep, just one more minute . . ."

Companies looking to harness the power of cartoons should keep the best practices of the medium in mind. Bring in cartoons to spotlight what's humorous about your brand, whether it's laugh-out-loud funny or witty. It's okay to poke a little fun at yourself or to mention events in pop culture that affect your industry and still remain on brand. If anything, doing this will humanize your company to your fans. Uncovering inspiration for what's funny about your company or your industry shouldn't be too hard. Simply visit your social media channels, speak with your customer service team, or host an internal brainstorm. Seed a few thought starters into the meeting, and watch the ideas fly!

When developing cartoons, keep in mind that they are an art form. So finding someone with a good drawing ability to bring your ideas to life is critical. The artwork doesn't need to be perfect, but the viewers need to be able to clearly identify what they're looking at.

The CEO of Get Satisfaction, Wendy Lea, partnered with Tom Fishburne, the marketoonist, to create a series of cartoons to market her company. Get Satisfaction is a community application that allows companies of all sizes to connect with their customers online, and that connection is facilitated by the company's software and managed and curated by clients' community managers.

When Ekaterina asked Lea why she chose cartoons to market her brand, Lea said:

> There are two reasons. We wanted to be creative, and we wanted that creativity to be memorable to a certain type of individual. In our case it was the community manager. Through cartoons we were trying to bring to the top of mind the challenges and the craziness community managers face in their daily jobs, as well as showcase both the demanding and the fun sides of their roles.

Get Satisfaction had created a lot of visual content, such as infographics, quite successfully in previous years, and the company wanted to stay within that visual lane to market its brand. But the company took the application of those visuals beyond ads. The company continues to use the 10-cartoon series from a content standpoint both online and offline. For example, the team designed cartoons into the posters and coasters to use and give away at their Customer Success Summit and around Customer Management Appreciation Day. The cartoons were a big hit and generated a lot of positive buzz for the company.

In the interview with the authors, Tom Fishburne said that there are several things that allow cartoons to stand out as a marketing vehicle. "One is the Trojan horse aspect of it: you can communicate an incredible amount of information in a very small space. Because it is couched in humor, and it is made very accessible, people like to see them. But then you can also carry in a message and an insight in the cartoon that conveys something deeper." Cartoon is an efficient communication device that allows viewers to break through the clutter. "I think the fact that cartoons can often work as a series is highly valuable," continues Fishburne. "It's not just a one-off piece of media; it's not like creating a YouTube video one time and hoping it goes viral. If there is some sort of cadence to a campaign in which you are releasing a new cartoon every so often, the audience starts to look out for them, and they want to find the next installment."

People like to laugh. That will always be a win with using cartoons as vehicles to deliver brand messages. But there is also a way of illustrating a need of the audience. "If you are marketing something, you are solving some sort of problem for that customer base," says Fishburne. "A cartoon does a good job of illustrating that self-need: how that audience feels that naturally sets up what you're trying to market as a solution for that. I think it works really well that the audience identifies themselves in the cartoons when they are reading them. They kind of put themselves into it, and that makes it much more personal and direct." Get Satisfaction's campaign most certainly showcased all of those aspects.

The challenge, obviously, is to do it in a way that the cartoons are not seen as infomercials, but instead as valuable pieces of content that people

genuinely want to see. And if you are successful, you will see amazing results. Fishburne says that some of his customers who use cartoons as regular content additions to their newsletters see an open rate of up to 45% on those e-mails versus the traditional open rate of 5 to 8%.

GIFs

While GIFs have been around since 1987, they're experiencing a new surge in popularity due to an uncanny ability to put an exclamation point on a moment. GIFs, or pictures in the Graphics Interchange Format, allow users to store multiple images or still frames from a video in an image file, bringing the image to life with animation. Though a relatively simple format at first glance, what makes GIFs special is their ability to tell a bite-sized story in a few seconds.

GIFs also stand out for the unique niche they've created for themselves in pop culture. Think about the witty jokes common in memes or the actions present in slapstick humor like a cream pie to the face or a dog chasing its tail. GIFs capture comical and funny moments in several seconds in a way that bridges the best of both photo and video. The end result is so addictive that consumers will share and watch GIFs over and over again.

Though GIFs have become pop culture darlings, there's plenty of creative potential for companies to tap in to. Over the Christmas holiday, Coca-Cola turned the "12 Days of Christmas," into the "12 Days of GIFs" to craft a seasonal story on its Tumblr blog. Inspired by the popular reaction blog *What Should We Call Me*, HBO's *Girls* created GIFs related to moments and themes from the show.

Although there's incredible potential for creativity, GIFs are supported on only certain platforms like Tumblr, Google+, blogs, and websites. GIFs have yet to break through on other platforms like Facebook, Twitter, and Pinterest. Sites like BuzzFeed and Mashable regularly run roundup articles with GIFs as the creatives. As a result, it seems like it's not a question of if but when GIFs will truly hit the mainstream social media.

Infographics

Infographics bring together the best of data and visuals to craft a story. Offering a visual representation of information, infographics help companies emphasize key points while packaging content in a highly shareable way. Infographics are understood and shared across social media platforms like Facebook, Twitter, Google+, and even Pinterest, where users create boards dedicated to the best infographics. When designed well, infographics can enhance thought leadership, educate a target audience, and optimize search engine rankings.

The beauty of infographics is that they can be designed around various data points on any topic. From how Google works to analyzing the growth of green technology or how to survive a zombie apocalypse, if there's valid, trustworthy data, there's potential for an infographic.

There have also been cases in which infographics haven't been shaped around numerical data. Instead, they focus on sharing expert information—for example, how-to steps, tips, and qualities, such as what your favorite ice cream flavor says about you. They can also communicate a top-10 list in a visual format.

A great example of an infographic that is both visual and useful is one designed by BRANDERATI in partnership with ShareRoot. It offers a meaningful list of metrics that brand marketers should track on Pinterest, and it explains each metric.

For more examples, visit sites like visual.ly, a site where designers and companies alike share infographics they've created.

Videos

When it comes to visual storytelling, the power of video is undeniable. Videos offer a compelling way for companies to stand out—and for good reason. From funny to educational, inspiring, surprising, motivational, or heartwarming, videos are personal, draw attention, and resonate with viewers in a way other mediums cannot. As Frank Eliason, SVP of Citibank says, "We tend to trust humans, not some corporate logo; and video is the best way to do that on a scaled basis."[7]

YouTube has been the grand dame of video since its inception in 2005—every minute in 2013, 100 hours of video footage was being uploaded, which was an increase of 100% from six years earlier.[8] Featuring videos of varying lengths, YouTube has become so respected for its video content that it now ranks second as a search engine to Google.[9] With sites like YouTube paving the way, the power of video continues to evolve in ways that make it easier, faster, and more cost effective for companies to produce and consumers to engage with. Apps like Vine, Instagram, Kik, and Viddy have evolved with consumer attention spans and preference for short-form video. These apps are available only on mobile devices, and they are meant to capture and share short-form video in real time. Sites like Pinterest and SlideShare now allow video in addition to pins and presentations. Platforms like Tongal have also popped up due to the demand from companies to crowdsource user-generated video content.

The popularity and variety of video platforms provides a prime opportunity to reach a large number of people and leave a lasting impression. In order to use video to connect with your customers on a deeper level, companies need to align their video goals with their audience needs. Companies also shouldn't be afraid of showing a little personality. No matter how well a video is produced, if your target audience doesn't find the information valuable, they won't watch or share the content. There also needs to be a strategy behind the mix of video content produced, in terms of types and platforms used. This strategy can be determined by the desired message, video length, consumer interest, and the company's ability to film and share in real time.

From Evian's dancing babies to the Old Spice Guy, companies have successfully extended the life of already popular advertising campaigns. When music phenomena like "Gangnam Style" and the "Harlem Shake" went viral, some companies joined in on the fun by filming their own parody videos. Companies have also used video to forge partnerships with celebrities or movie phenomena, such as when Pringles joined forces with *Star Wars* to host a crowdsourced video contest with its fans to channel "The Force for Fun."

Pinterest

metrics marketers should consider tracking:

BROUGHT TO YOU BY:

BRANDERATI @shareroot

IMPRESSIONS

The number of times pins from your brand's website were seen each day on Pinterest.

PIN REACH

The number of people on Pinterest who saw a pin from your brand's website each day on Pinterest.

CLICKS

The number of clicks pins from your brand's website received each day.

MOST RECENT

This pin feed shows you the most recent pins that originated from your brand's website.

AVERAGE REPINS PER PIN

Based on your brand's previous engagement history, average repins per pin, defines the average repins your brand has received each time it has made a pin or a repin.

AVERAGE LIKES PER PIN

Based on your brand's previous engagement history, average likes per pin defines the average likes your brand has received each time it has made a pin or a repin.

AVERAGE COMMENTS PER PIN

Based on your brand's previous engagement history, average comments per pin defines the average comments your brand has received each time it has made a pin or a repin.

AVERAGE 2ND DEGREE FOLLOWERS

Average 2nd degree followers shows your brand how connected your follower base is. Specifically the average number of followers each of your brand's followers has.

MOST REPINNED

This pin feed shows you the most repinned pins that originated from your brand's website.

MOST CLICKED

This pin feed shows you the most clicked on pins that originated from your brand's website.

TOP FANS AND INFLUENCERS

A list of the most influential and most connected Pinterest users following your brand.

TOP PINS

Pins originating from your brand's website with the most engagement.

TOP INTERACTIONS

Total Pinterest interactions with all of the pins originating from content on your brand's website.

FOLLOWERS ENGAGEMENT

Follower engagement percentage shows your brand what percentage of your follower base you can expect to engage with each of your pins/repins.

SHORT TERM FOLLOWER ENGAGEMENT

A current/recent snapshot of follower engagement. Your short term follower engagement will fluctuate rapidly in comparison to follower engagement, and is best used to measure the effectiveness of a recent modification to your brand's Pinterest strategy.

REACH

Reach shows your brand the number of unique newsfeed impressions you can expect each time you make a pin or repin.

VELOCITY

Current average number of pins/repins your brand makes per week. This metric is a great tool for testing out the ideal amount of pins/repins your brand should be pinning per week. If you modify the velocity and keep it steady at a modified rate, you can use the "short term follower engagement" metric to determine whether the change in velocity produced better engagement results for your brand.

Videos can also help companies to take fans behind the scenes during major events. For example, fashion retailer TopShop partnered with Google+ to live stream its AW13 fashion show from the models' perspective. Tiny cameras were hidden in the models' clothes so the viewers could watch and feel what it was like to strut down the runway at a major fashion show. TopShop also used Vine to share moments from the show and exclusive behind-the-scenes video content.

Companies have also used video to communicate an important platform or inspirational mission. In Dove's *Real Beauty Sketches*, women are asked to describe their facial features for a forensic artist. A stranger who has recently met the same women is also asked to describe their features to the artist. In the end, the women see two very different photos, which dramatically shows the importance of how we look at ourselves. The story of encouraging confidence and feeling beautiful is powerful and incredibly shareable, with 56 million views on YouTube and counting.[10]

The continued volume of video content, combined with the surge in new ways to capture and stream in real time, paints a bright future. Companies that have struggled to find resources or define a video strategy should embrace the wave of creativity, platforms, and tools available. As the trend indicates, it will continue to get easier and more seamless to incorporate video into your visual storytelling program.

Presentations

Social and online media have reinvented how we look at presentations. Presentations are no longer just for conferences, speeches, and business meetings. Presentations have become an art form, with highly visual layouts, content, and snappy bits of text. With creative titles and a defined flow of information, the slide-by-slide navigation of a presentation offers a dynamic visual storytelling opportunity—all without the need for a speaker.

Presentations can be housed on company websites, blogs, or platforms like SlideShare that boast a massive following and facilitate easy sharing across popular social media platforms. Inspiration for presentations can come from anywhere, including executive speeches, blog entries, webinars, case studies, white papers, infographics, new product launches, how-tos, lists, company events, and more.

The key when dreaming up new presentation ideas is to think creatively and listen to your community. The vast majority of people are visual learners, so think of your presentations as an opportunity for networking, thought leadership, and consumer engagement. What can you capture in a highly visual format to motivate, inspire, or teach? Consider frequently asked questions coming into your social media or customer service team or perhaps an internal speech to motivate employees. Aggregation of niche statistics, quotes, facts, and so on can also make a valuable resource for your target audience. Humor can also be used in presentations, as seen by HubSpot's "12 Terrible (but funny) Places to Work" or GoToMeeting's "10 Reasons Geeks Make the Best Mates."

When Ekaterina Walter, coauthor of this book, was marketing her first book *Think Like Zuck: The Five Business Secrets of Facebook's Improbably Brilliant CEO Mark Zuckerberg,* she put together a visual collection of the 12 most interesting quotes by Mark Zuckerberg featured in her book. The presentation was viewed so many times that it was featured on SlideShare's home page, and it has had over 97,000 organic views to date, with no promotional dollars behind it.

In order to set your presentations apart, spend time developing a design aesthetic and voice for your company. Determine what sides of your company's personality you want to show, plus key stories that you can bring to life. Make sure to build storyboards for your presentations that make each slide a key supporting point in the overall story.

The best presentations favor a clean, easy-to-follow layout. You want your layout, text, and visuals all to work together, versus competing for attention. SlideShare presentations have an average of 19 slides and 19 images, which means that there's about one photo per slide.[11] Slides now contain an average of 24 words per slide, indicating a focus on high-impact stats, statements, quotes, and visuals.[12] It's also important that your end slide be branded to your company and encourage sharing, e-mail opt-in, following your channel, and so on.

As companies continue to embrace the power of visual content, the ability to package different stories, ideas, and campaigns into a presentation will remain a valuable tool in your arsenal.

Aggregators

With so much content on the web and social media sites, it's easy to feel overwhelmed when trying to source the most shareworthy content. In response to the never-ending stream of content, aggregators have boomed in popularity to help both people and companies organize and share important information. Aggregators offer access to timely, relevant content, and they can be curated according to your company's interests. Although many aggregators are link based, the rise of visual content has resulted in a wave of aggregators that cater to images, videos, and more.

Paper.li is a free and useful tool for creating a visual online newspaper in minutes with content that has been crowdsourced from articles, photos, and videos across the Internet. Companies can pull in content from their Facebook, Twitter, and Google+ pages, plus popular newspapers. The end result delivers relevant content based on timely subjects of interest from your company and industry. Consider developing a custom Paper.li for a major event leveraging the event hashtag, so you can pull in all of the important tweets, photos, videos, and blog content into a great takeaway to share postevent. More custom Pro accounts are also available for a fee.

On the next page is Ekaterina's Paper.li digital newspaper *The Social Media News Daily* that automatically goes out to all her Twitter followers on a daily basis and serves as a great subject of regular Twitter conversations and is a fantastic relationship building tool for the author.

RebelMouse is another free aggregation tool that connects all of your social media activity and live streams it in a highly visual way that's similar to Pinterest on a personalized website. There are so many options for integration—if you can dream it up, you can probably find a way to get it on your RebelMouse site. Options listed include RSS feeds, custom hashtags, Twitter, Facebook, Google+, Instagram, LinkedIn, Tumblr, Pinterest, YouTube accounts, and more. It's free, but your domain will be www.rebelmouse.com/username. For a fee, custom domains can be purchased.

In the enterprise space, aggregators aim to provide a seamless experience for sharing amazing user-generated content through branded content. The difference is that customized content can be sourced and integrated in real time across a number of online and offline platforms from websites to Facebook tabs, TV, mobile sites, digital screens, and more. Two of the major players include MassRelevance and Postano. Both offer the ability to create a slick, branded experience that pulls in visual content and conversations across all major social networks and Internet sources. The end goal is to let your fans tell the story of your

brand through a continuous steam of shareable visuals.

Using MassRelevance, for example, Pepsi turned its home page into an interactive pop culture dashboard with a Live for Now theme driven by fan-generated images on social media.

Intel went one step further and in 2012 launched a mobile-first, employee-curated digital magazine called *iQ*, the digital newsstand that aggregates the best stories from the Internet about technology. It looks like Flipboard, aggregates content like Reddit, and serves up news visually, like Newsmap.

As an ingredient brand, Intel touches almost every part of the technical modern world. Given that, the *iQ* editorial strategy is to narrate those touch points that may get overlooked or to tell stories on innovation everywhere from an Intel point of view.

Beyond this "brand as publisher" exercise, Intel *iQ* is quickly transforming itself to be part of a wider "brand as publishing network." Through partnerships with publishers such as PSFK, BuzzFeed, Vice, and others, *iQ*'s original and cocreated content syndicates throughout publishing networks and touch points like Flipboard and Zite. Intel also uses this content in paid distribution services like Outbrain and Sharethrough.

iQ has become the hub for Intel's social content and strategy. Once content lands on *iQ*, it is then available in a form that is optimized for Intel's owned social properties, like Facebook, Twitter, and Tumblr. The company is increasingly integrating it with paid media, and it has plans to take it global in key markets in 2014.

With the rise of visual storytelling, expect to see the range of tools and service providers in the content aggregator space continue to grow. It's always been a challenge to track and monitor a multitude of social media channels, e-mail newsletter subscriptions, and RSS feeds, warranting the demand for automating the delivery of relevant content in a visual package. The challenge for companies will be to focus on curation versus merging all of their outbound content in one place. The use of social media is ultimately about the power of your community, so the experience needs to feel personal versus automated. The more that companies can use aggregators to discover inspiring visual content that sparks a conversation and engagement, the better.

Types of Images Used for Visual Storytelling

Photography

- Any moment can turn into a photo opportunity.
- Photos people share across social media platforms show what's important to them and what they believe is shareworthy.
- Well-composed photos are not new to companies; however social media–friendly images that drive an immediate response are!
- On social media, users look for realistic photos and brand-aligned images.

Graphs and Drawings

- For highly technical products, graphs and visualizations can be a better option.
- Many are visual learners and respond better to charts, graphs, and numbers.
- In some cases, easy-to-read visuals make messages more digestible and more sharable.

User-Generated Images

- Collaborative storytelling can deepen relationships with consumers.
- Consider developing a user-generated image program.
- When consumers are part of the process, incredible images can come out of collaborative storytelling programs.
- Collaborative storytelling benefits both customers and companies. Customers get to see their images liked by fans, and companies get insight on what motivates customers.

Photo Collages

- Multiple images and collages can sometimes tell stories better than one image alone.
- It is an easy concept! Many times tens, or even hundreds, of photos and images are being shared, and combining them may help tell a visual story.
- Multiple images offer a creative opportunity to highlight different attributes of a company, a product, or an event.

Images with Text Overlays: Captions, Quotes, and Stats

- These images are a cost effective and easy way to enhance a traditional image.
- They are also a great way to make sure captions aren't overlooked.
- Small amounts of text, one-liners, quotes, or stats, can greatly contribute to your visual story.

Types of Images Used for Visual Storytelling, continued

Postcards and E-cards

- Postcards aren't dead! They've been reinvented by the Internet as a way to put photos and text together.
- E-cards are highly sharable. Whether on a social media platform such as Pinterest or in a brand's campaign, e-cards are a great opportunity for unique storytelling.

Word Photos

- Words can be images too!
- Tools such as WordPhoto (iPhone/iPad app) and WordCam Pro (Android app) can create compelling visual images out of everything from taglines to buzzwords.

Memes

- Memes are ideas that spread from person to person, and they serve to spread cultural information.
- Memes can be jokes, phrases, concepts, images, videos, and pop culture that are extremely sharable.
- Popular meme examples are: "I can has cheezburger," "Success Kid," "Hipster Ariel," and "Bachelor Frog."
- Brands have started using memes as tools for awareness and social proof.

Cartoons

- Cartoons are a powerful visual storytelling tool because they can be funny, artistic, and engaging all in one.
- Cartoons are known for being a funny and delightful way to visually spread stories.
- Cartoons can trigger brand recognition and nostalgia, which makes them a compelling storytelling medium.
- Great ideas for cartoons can come from customers, pop culture, promotions, fun facts, products, or anywhere else!

GIFs

- GIFs (Graphics Interchange Format) bring multiple images and still frames from a video to life via animation.
- GIFs are a great example of visual storytelling because they tell bite-sized stories in only a few seconds.
- A medium between photo and video, GIFs capture funny moments in an instant.

Infographics

- Infographics are visual representations of information, bringing together the data and visuals to tell a story.

(continued)

Types of Images Used for Visual Storytelling, *continued*

Infographics, *continued*
- Infographics can highlight key ideas that are highly visual and shareable.
- They crop up across social media, from Facebook to Twitter, Google+, and Pinterest. Entire Pinterest boards are dedicated to great infographics.
- A well-designed infographic can affect thought leadership, inform target audiences, and optimize search engine rankings.
- Infographics are extremely versatile and can be designed for data on any topic.

Videos
- Videos help companies and brands reach consumers in a way that no other visual mediums can.
- Videos can tell a visual story that's funny, inspiring, personal, heartwarming, and they also highlight a product, an idea, or a brand image.
- YouTube is one example of a site that increasingly makes it easy and cost-effective for companies to create and share with consumers.
- Social apps such as Vine, Instagram, Kik, and Viddy offer an avenue for short-form videos.

- Sites such as Pinterest and SlideShare allow video in addition to pins and presentations.
- Crowdsourced user-generated video platforms, such as Tongal, are also in demand.

Presentations
- Presentations are more visual than ever before and are no longer just for the conference room.
- Today's presentations are highly visual, artistic, and engaging.
- Slide-by-slide information, defined flow of information, and creative titles have reinvented presentations to the point where speakers aren't even necessary.
- Platforms such as Slideshare, individual company websites, and blogs offer the opportunity to make presentations sharable and build social followings.
- A creative presentation can be inspired by anything, from executive speeches to blog entries, and are a dynamic visual storytelling opportunity.

The Seven Elements of Visual Storytelling

Similar to how people grow relationships with each other, visual storytelling offers companies meaningful opportunities to deliver positive experiences that build brand awareness, trust, loyalty, and engaged communities.

In order to develop and implement a successful visual storytelling strategy, marketers must focus on the following elements:

1 Design

2 Personalization

3 Usefulness

4 Personality

5 Storytelling

6 Shareworthiness

7 Real-time amplification

Embrace Visual Imagery

When it comes to the design element of visual marketing, it's inspiring to see companies curating stunning imagery with the help of talented artists and photographers. One company that does this exceptionally well is Land Rover USA, with its Tumblr blog *The Journey* (http://tumblr.landroverusa .com). Featuring gorgeous photos, such as the "ferocious" photo of a beautiful animal, the tiger, all images in *The Journey* come together to tell an aspirational story of the Land Rover brand targeted at rugged and romantic adventurers.

Taken by photographer Jay Trinidad for Land Rover, these images underscore how capturing stunning, yet powerful visual imagery can tell a story and add to the overall branding of the vehicle, without the use of text. The image of a tiger in front of a vehicle, for example, is highly stylized, which speaks to the quality and luxury of the car, and the roaring statue of the animal showcases that this high-end vehicle has the heart and prowess of the tiger. While the Tumblr post does include text that says "FEROCIOUS. And fearless," it is easily conveyed through the image.

Personalize, Don't Spray

Another key theme of visual marketing is the personalization of content by platform. Gone are the days when it's okay to spray the same piece of content across multiple platforms. Instead, social media leaders are embracing the special features and capabilities of each type of platform to foster different types of engagement and storytelling.

General Electric is a great example of a company that adopts unique strategies for visual marketing across different platforms. Whether it's Facebook, Tumblr, Instagram, Pinterest, Vine, or YouTube, the content is different, but it is consistent across the themes of science, technology, and innovation. One of General Electric's unique approaches to visual content can be found on Pinterest, which showcases incredibly creative boards (http://www.pinterest.com/generalelectric). With the goal of inspiring people to build, power, move, and cure the world, the board titles include "Badass Machines," "#GEInspiredMe," "Mind = Blown," and more. There's even a little geek humor found in a board called "Hey Girl," which shares spoof pick-up lines from Thomas Edison.

Make Yourself Useful

By playing off of the strengths of each social media platform, companies are taking the first step in ensuring that their visual content is also useful. However, personalization alone does not necessarily make content useful. Social listening can help companies be more useful and relevant by uncovering key themes and trends around which to craft visual content. Social listening can also help companies to better understand what drives consumers and prompts action, whether it's sharing, engaging, or purchasing.

Whole Foods is a good example of a company that goes above and beyond in being useful and relevant to its consumers. The company has more than 600 social media accounts, spanning both the national and store levels. Local stores are tasked with developing content related to what's happening, or being offered, much of which is visual across sites like Facebook, Pinterest, and Instagram. At the national level, sites like Pinterest help Whole Foods be useful at scale (http://www.pinterest.com/wholefoods). Clearly, it's not a leap to assume that a grocery store offering recipe content would offer value. However, Whole Foods Market has become a leader on Pinterest for its unique approach to cocreation.

During the Visual Voice panel at SXSW 2013, Whole Foods' director of social media, Natanya Anderson, shared that for every pin, Whole Foods repins five things from other people, making sure that they're able to appropriately source and credit the content. Whole Foods also participates in cocreation by bringing in different subject matter experts to help them pin worthwhile content. As a result, Pinterest has overtaken all of Whole Foods' other social media channels for traffic generation to the recipes on WholeFoodsMarket.com. During the panel, Anderson went as far as to say that Pinterest's 110,000 followers generate 15 times more value than Facebook and Twitter combined. For example, one of the most popular Pinterest recipes for spaghetti squash has been repinned 68,000 times, driving 44,000 views to the recipe on Whole Foods' website.[13]

Be Human

In addition to being useful, visual marketing performs better when the content has a human element. Being human means feeling more like a friend than a corporate entity. A friend has a personality, values the relationship, shares experiences, and understands when to listen, when to be serious, and when to have fun. Being human means not leading with "buy this now." Instead of going straight for the sell on social media sites, companies need to think through how people discuss and recommend a product or service to a friend. Evaluate and learn from the best practices of known influencers and superfans who are producing trustworthy visual content about your company. Chances are, you'll find that the trust is generated in part because of their reputation but also because they discuss and share product attributes in a relatable, easy-to-understand way.

It's also important to go beyond what people are saying about your company and understand what else they care about. Learn what issues, causes, and interests are important to them, plus what motivates them. For example, if your customer base is passionate about sports or entertainment, content can be crafted around a major event, season, and more. This is strategic because people aren't going on social media sites to hear from companies. They are hopping onto Facebook to see their cousin's vacation photos or to post photos from a birthday party. Being human also means fitting in, so your goal as a company is to craft visual content that's a welcome interruption between the status updates, photos, and more that people come on social media platforms to view.

One way to show the more human side of your company is by putting your community's user-generated content in the spotlight. In Lululemon's #TheSweatLife campaign (http://thesweatlife.lululemon.com), the company prompted its fans to share on Twitter or Instagram how they get their sweat on for a chance to appear on the company's website or social media channels. It used a service called Olapic, which offers software for collecting user-generated photos across Facebook, Twitter, and Instagram. Naturally, the photos all put Lululemon apparel in the spotlight, but it did so in a way that personified the brand and the people who live an active, healthy lifestyle. Lululemon could craft a ton of inspiring visual content to promote its brand, but seeing real people out living their lives while wearing the company's apparel is more relatable. People could see how the clothing fits on real bodies and not just on models. They could also use the images to source styling ideas, fitness tips, and more. According to an interview with Nancy Richardson, Lululemon's vice president of digital and brand strategy, the campaign launched in fall 2012 and, as of spring 2013, there had been more than 26,000 people who had used #thesweatlife hashtag on Instagram, plus over 2 million page views on Lululemon's website.[14]

Tell a Story

All of the visual marketing examples thus far prove that a successful visual marketing strategy requires that the content's storytelling element be just as important as the use of the visuals. Stories can come from a number of places, whether it's company values, how people enjoy your products or services, key milestones, or simply by being timely and relevant. For example, in Oreo's Daily Twist campaign, the company celebrated its one hundredth birthday by developing 100 compelling images inspired by real-time pop culture (http://www.pinterest.com/oreo/daily-twist). Holidays and timely occasions celebrated included National Talk Like a Pirate Day, Hispanic Heritage Month, the Mars Rover landing, and more. While each piece of content was different, the creative theme of showcasing a unique twist on pop culture happenings and holidays for an extended window of time added a storytelling element. The campaign ultimately garnered global praise and awards, and it redefined how many people looked at the Oreo brand.

Be Shareworthy in Everything You Do

Akin to lightning in a bottle, companies and brands of all sizes are looking for similar visual storytelling opportunities to hit those magical high notes with their consumers. According to Coca-Cola, one way to do this is by being shareworthy in everything you do. Wendy Clark, SVP of integrated marketing communications and capabilities for Coca-Cola, told *Fortune*, "For Coca-Cola, our Facebook fans are just over one fan or friend away from the entire Facebook community of 1 billion+. So if we do our job well of developing useful, compelling, interesting, and shareworthy content, our fans become our sales force for us."[15]

Clark also encourages companies to think of their customers as storytellers: "Taking the principle of Initial and Ultimate audiences, we're increasingly thinking about all of our constituents as storytellers, not just receivers of our content."[16] Clark cites that as much as 80% of conversation about the Coca-Cola brand comes from its customers, offering opportunities for cocreation, versus simply pushing out messages and hoping they will stick.

STATS

According to BuzzFeed, every minute 208,300 photos are posted to Facebook, 27,800 photos are shared on Instagram, 510,000 photos are liked on Instagram, and 100 hours of video are being uploaded to YouTube.[17]

An example of how Coca-Cola is embracing its customers as storytellers can be found in its #BestSummerMoment campaign. Hosted on a microsite and the company's social media channels including Facebook, Twitter, and Instagram, Coca-Cola encouraged its customers to share their unforgettable summer moments. Coca-Cola celebrated its fans by sharing some of the best photos across its microsite and social media channels, plus offering some lucky participants a special reward to open even more summer moments. During the #BestSummerMoment campaign, the company sourced incredible photos to use on its social media channels, including a collage of newly-weds enjoying Coca-Cola on their honeymoon and many more. Many of the photos submitted were highly shareable, and they told a unique and emotional story that was a positive reflection of the Coca-Cola brand.

Live in the Moment

There's a massive amount of visual and video content for consumers to sort through. There's also a lot of opportunity for real-time interaction and engagement. Think back to the Introduction to Ekaterina's example with Benefit: the company quickly tweeted her an image of a compliment to put a smile on her face during the tough day. Developing a robust image and video library filled with content to share in real time offers companies a strong opportunity to add value in the moment. The challenges and opportunities, which will be discussed in depth in Chapter 4, are how to anticipate the types of content you'll need.

In addition to daily consumer engagement, living in the moment also extends to current events. From the news of the day, to traditional and wacky holidays, or a meme that just went viral, there's no shortage of topics to pull from. The key is to stay aligned with your company's values and to play to your strengths. Oh, and you never, ever, want to look like you're marketing to a tragic event. For example, as the eyes of the world turned to the Boston Marathon bombing tragedy during April 2013, Scott Monty, head of global social media for Ford Motor Company, tweeted, "If you manage social media for a brand, this would be a good time to suspend any additional posts for the day." The companies who ceased their planned communications and posted heartfelt messages about Boston were rewarded, while those who appeared to be marketing to the disaster lost fans and suffered a blow to their reputation.

An example of being timely without being promotional happened in February 2013 when a massive blizzard hit Boston. With people stuck at home, two Boston-area sports teams, the New England Patriots and the Boston Red Sox, revised their content calendars to focus on what people would be buzzing about—the snowstorm. From the beloved Boston Red Sox mascot, Wally the Green Monster, waist deep in snow digging out Fenway Park, to the New England Patriots' showing fan photos of snowmen dressed up in team gear, both teams were relevant and fun in real time without being promotional. The teams showed their fans that they too were digging out and having fun in the snow, and they were rewarded with engagement, positive comments, and fans' sharing their content. The Boston Red Sox tweeted a picture of Wally shoveling the snow with the message: "Wally is still digging out. . . . Are you?"

In the next chapter we will dive deeper into each social network and provide tips and case studies for each. In Chapter 4 we will walk you through developing a visual storytelling road map and show you how to implement it.

The Power of the Platform: Visual Storytelling on Social Networks

n today's world of information consumption, we're surrounded by media, and it's never been more important to grab your audience's attention with high-quality content. The brain processes visual content 60,000 times faster than text[1] so it is no wonder that marketers are increasingly turning to strong visual content to engage their audiences—and keep their attention.

The average adult attention span has been shown to be somewhere between 2.8 and 8 seconds; marketers need to get their message across quickly and effectively.[2]

Social media have made it easy for brands to connect with customers not just through text but with photos, videos, infographics, and other images. This chapter will show just what a vital role visual marketing is playing in brands' social media strategies and its impact on engagement and sales. Visual media are increasingly being used instead of text by marketers keen to connect with customers—and to have their messages amplified with shares, likes, and comments.

Too many companies opt for a blanket coverage approach to social media. They share the same posts in the same way to all channels, and then they question why their followers aren't engaging with their content. There isn't a one-size-fits-all solution to social media: each network has its own character and audience. To get the most out of your social media channels, you need to create strong content—and then use it to start a conversation that is appropriate to that network.

In this chapter we're going to take a look at how to get the most out of some of the most popular networks for sharing visual content: how to use that content to engage your audience, how to build it in to your campaigns, and how to make your brand stand out above the chatter.

> The people in your audience don't want to be broadcasted *to*: they want to be part of a conversation—and to feel like you're listening.

Social media are increasingly offering solutions to the demise of traditional marketing and the fragmentation of our attention across so many channels. We're going to look at how some of the most successful brands have used the visual strengths of social media to grab their audience's attention—and to keep it.

Pinterest

The dark horse of the social media race is surely the image-community site Pinterest. On the surface, Pinterest is a whimsical pinboarding site where members share their favorite images and photos, grouped around themes. Users can follow pinboards or whole profiles and repin images to their own boards, adding comments and likes.

Pinterest's meteoric rise in only a few years shows that the site is more than just a pretty community for people interested in fashion and lifestyle. Marketers are all over Pinterest's lead-generation aspects, because online hits on products from the site have proved a marketing sensation.

Pinterest Facts and Figures

- This image sharing network was cofounded by Iowa's Ben Silbermann, and it was launched in March 2010.
- By August 2011 it had already made it onto *Time* Magazine's "50 Best Websites for 2011" list.
- CNN called Pinterest "2012's hottest website," after unique visitors to the site grew 400% from September to December 2011.
- Pinterest now drives more referral traffic than Google+, YouTube, and LinkedIn combined.[3]
- Pinterest's user base is only 7% of Twitter's, but the platform sends more total referral traffic than Twitter.[4]
- With a mere 1% of Facebook's user count, Pinterest sends 13% of the traffic that Facebook does.[5]
- 80% of users are female, and lifestyle, hobby, crafts, and design are the most popular themes.[6]
- 50% of all Pinterest users have children.[7]
- By February 2013, Pinterest had 25 million users.[8]
- Sephora says its Pinterest followers spend 15 times more than their Facebook fans.[9]
- 82% of fashion- and retail-related images are being pinned by the community, with brands' pinning only 18% of content.[10]

- 70% of brand engagement on Pinterest is generated by users, not by brands.[11]
- Top brands in the fashion and retail space average 46 repins on every pin.[12]
- U.S. consumers who use Pinterest follow an average of 9.3 retailers on the site.[13]
- Pinterest pins that include prices receive 36% more likes than those that do not.[14]
- Moms are 61% more likely to visit Pinterest than the average American.[15]
- 81% of U.S. online consumers trust information and advice from Pinterest.[16]
- Pinterest accounts for 25% of retail referral traffic.[17]
- Over 80% of pins are repins.[18]
- The average Pinterest user spends 98 minutes per month on the site, compared to 2.5 hours on Tumblr and 7 hours on Facebook.[19]
- Out of 17 million brand engagements, 15% occurred on the brand's boards and 85% occurred elsewhere on Pinterest.[20]
- 83.9% of a pinner's time is spent Pinning, while 15.5% is spent liking and 0.6% is spent leaving comments.[21]
- 57% of Pinterest users interact with food-related content, the number one category of content.[22]

According to a study by Shareaholic, the site now drives more referral traffic than Google+, YouTube, and LinkedIn combined.[23]

Although it is most known for photographs, you can also pin images such as infographics, cartoons, artwork, or short, visual quotes. You can add videos, too, which many companies use to give short tutorials or how-to style guidance.

Pinterest's slick, clean look is dominated by images and videos. When you go to a user's profile, you see his or her themed boards, all beautifully arranged. Each board may contain many pins, and these can be commented on and liked, but the text is definitely secondary to the images.

"Pinterest Is Worth $2 Billion Because Its 25 Million Users Are Rich, Female, and Like to Spend." This headline from *Business Insider*[24] sums up what the savvy marketer knows already: one of the most sought-after consumer groups, women, particularly householders, are spending an increasing amount of time on Pinterest, and they are using it as a venue for their online shopping. Brands who don't have a presence on the site are losing out, both in terms of sales and in terms of potential new customer demographics.

Although it's known for being the site of choice for the lifestyle and fashion industries, Pinterest can help all industries find new audiences and connect with their fans through images. The U.S. Army, for instance, has a hugely popular page with boards that feature Army values, families, veterans, history—and, of course, Army style!

It's all about translation: finding ways to appeal to Pinterest users, even if you don't think your brand is a natural fit for the site. Digital news magazine *Mashable*'s site has one of the largest followings on Pinterest with almost 1.5 million fans, despite the fact that the brand doesn't fall into any of the more usual fashion or style categories (http://www.pinterest.com/mashable). It does, however, feature pinboards for "The Modern Kitchen," "Nerdy Desserts," and "Fashion Meets Digital." There is a little bit of something for everyone with boards like "Gorgeous Instagram Photos," "Pets Gone Digital," "3D Printing Creations," "Women in Tech," and "Web Humor." The digital news magazine has done a great job hitting on exactly the right format to appeal to the Pinterest ethos: finding a visual way to represent its brand in a fun, humorous, and stylish manner. Marketers just have to think outside the box a little to find innovative ways to reach the Pinterest audience, but by getting the formula right, they can reach large, new, untapped audiences.

Pinterest's format makes it very easy to share images, and it provides excellent lead generation, especially for visual industries. Because Pinterest users can add a widget to their desktop that allows them to easily repin images from any website onto their own Pinterest boards, companies who haven't even got a profile on Pinterest have discovered new traffic coming in from the site from fans repinning images from the company website. Images taken from a site will still link back to the original source, so as long as they come from your website, you can still see a boost in your traffic coming from Pinterest.

It is better to add your own Pinterest button on your website so you don't lose out from users' finding your photos from other sources, such as Internet searches. Make it easy for fans to repin your images directly, especially if you have an image-rich site.

Those who don't think of their websites in terms of optimizing them for Pinterest are missing the chance to share their products with a brand-loyal audience with disposable income. The brand agency Digitas says that automotive brands in particular are missing the boat: "Unlike the fashion/retail brands, top automotive brands average 3 repins on every pin, while the community receives 10 repins per pin. One reason the automotive industry might be seeing lower engagement on Pinterest than other industries is because most current automotive sites are structured to use Flash, which makes it difficult for users to pin content."[25]

Even for nonvisual industries, Pinterest users (generally young, female, educated, and affluent) are often a key demographic that marketers want to reach, and the site provides an excellent opportunity to interact with them in a completely different way than traditional advertising allows.

The site's community and sharing features give you the chance to have your message distributed by your followers (or their followers, or *their* followers . . .) to a potentially large audience of activated, social, brand-loyal users. These are exactly the types of people who make for the best brand advocates: they share, like, and comment on images from their network, and they are highly motivated to find out more about your products by clicking on the images to find the source.

If we have a look at Pinterest's core demographic—women (80%), especially moms, with disposable income—we can see the hard-to-reach groups that marketers are often failing to engage with their traditional advertising (91% of women in one survey said that advertisers don't understand them).[26] As women account for 85% of all consumer purchases including everything from autos to healthcare, it is essential for marketers to find new ways of targeting them.[27] Pinterest offers a creative solution to this problem for marketers who are willing to think about innovative ways of representing their brand through images and who want to engage with fans and new audiences online.

Creativity is at the center of Pinterest's design. Choosing themes for your boards can open your company up to a whole world of ideas for visually interpreting its brand. We have compiled the following collection of board name and theme ideas that hopefully will get you excited and help you get started.

Some of the ideas for a company's Pinterest board names and themes include these:

Inspiration and Ideas

1. Holiday ideas
2. Seasonal boards
3. Spring, summer, fall, or winter style
4. In your home
5. Customer photos
6. Party ideas

TIPS *for Engaging on Pinterest*

- If you want followers to engage with your pins, make sure to like, follow, repin, and comment on other people's images. Pinterest makes it easy for you: the more people and boards you follow, the more ideas you will have for pins to share.
- Pinterest is all about creativity and having fun, so think about the lighter side of your brand. Southwest Airlines has boards for plane-related crafts and plane party ideas.
- Create images for marketing with Pinterest in mind. For example, each blog post should have a strong image that can be shared on Pinterest to amplify your message.
- Your boards should stand out if they are going to attract followers. Choosing a strong theme and great images are obviously central to this, but so is giving it a snappy title to attract people's attention.
- Images don't have to be professionally shot, but use images that are colorful, well balanced, and interesting.
- Add "Pin it!" and other social sharing buttons to your website, so your fans can spread the word.
- Find ways to involve fans—perhaps a competition in which fans create their own memes or send in pictures of themselves using your product.
- Decide on the story you want to tell with your images.
- Focus on your customers. What images would they find useful, entertaining, and inspiring?
- YouTube videos can be pinned to boards in the same way as any other thumbnail, so you can show off your expertise with how-to videos for aspects of your business.
- Show behind the scenes at your company with boards about your staff, local environment, and industry, or find other ways to use interesting images to help people find out about what you offer.
- Make use of what is possible with the Pinboard format by putting together looks and lifestyle ideas, or show your products in real environments to show how they can work.
- Pinterest has a very current format: popular images often reflect seasonal trends or events, such as holidays (Valentine's Day and others) or movie releases.
- Popularity on Pinterest comes from shedding a typical "brand" profile and really getting behind the network's ethos.

7 Around the world

8 Tech ideas

9 Things we love

10 Color-themed boards: white, red, and blue

11 Upcoming

12 Exercise and activity

13 Health

14 Back to school

15 Thank you!

16 Social media

17 Home and kitchen

18 Fashion

19 Humor

20 Brand-themed weddings

21 Toys and games

22 Quotes

23 Environment and eco-friendly themes

24 Charities or good causes

25 Retro boards: images from the past

Information About Your Company and Its products

1 Webinars

2 Infographics

3 Videos

4 Deals and offers

5 Shop

6 Store locations; about our stores

7 How-to videos and photos

8 Our ads

9 In the news

10 Upcoming events

11 Conferences

12 Product demonstrations

13 Getting started

14 Help and advice

15 Troubleshooting

16 Style ideas: how our product fits into a lifestyle

17 Budget ideas: low-cost ideas for presents or styles

Information About Your Brand

1 Heritage

2 Behind the scenes

3 Our team

4 Our sponsored event

5 Have your say (customer-uploaded ideas)

6 Our offices

7 Our favorite foods

8 The office party

9 When we were young (baby photos of staff)

10 Our customers

11 Our clients

12 Our mission

13 Our company's charity

14 Our community

15 Our town

16 Fan Love

Pinterest can boost traffic to websites from a whole range of businesses and for companies of all sizes. Louisville resident Kim Gordon and her 15-year-old daughter Chloe created the PopCosmo site in 2011 as a trend-spotting site for teens showing off the latest fashion, beauty, makeup, and lifestyle tips. Immediately they saw the value in Pinterest as a way to generate interest in their site (http://www.pinterest.com/popcosmo). Chloe runs the social media platforms for PopCosmo, and her content focuses on providing visual inspiration and useful DIY tutorials—both types of media Pinterest users love. Her images for the PopCosmo site and social media pages focus on helping teens stay trendy in fun, creative ways. According to Kim, Pinterest accounts for half of the referral traffic to PopCosmo and 20% of the site's overall traffic.

"When a pin goes viral," says Kim, "it can alter our web stats for months."

And Kim and Chloe's visual storytelling savvy doesn't just extend to their own Pinboard—they encourage their readers to spread the word about their site through images.

One article on their site, a tutorial on creating French manicures, has been pinned over 380,000 times, and that's not even including likes or repins.

You don't necessarily need a big marketing budget to be successful on Pinterest, but you need to put some effort into thinking about how your brand relates to Pinterest users, and you need to be willing to engage with fans.

Melanie Duncan is a female entrepreneur whose business is booming thanks to Pinterest. It's hard to believe that earlier this year she didn't even know the site existed!

Melanie owns Luxury Monograms—a website specializing in monogrammed décor and gifts. Her product range includes throw pillows, tableware, towels, shower curtains, and apparel featuring bold monograms in a variety of styles. At some point she noticed a huge spike in traffic to her site: "When I logged in to my analytics account, I was shocked to see that Pinterest had become my site's number one traffic referral source, above Google and Facebook. But what was even more exciting was that the traffic was converting. I was getting thousands of dollars in sales and thousands of new visitors to my site each month just from others pinning my products on Pinterest. Once I realized the opportunity, I created an account for my business, and I began to develop marketing strategies for using it."

Melanie's boards are a mix of product pictures and general décor and apparel inspiration (http://www.pinterest.com/luxurymonograms): "For example, I sell entertaining items like placemats and napkins. I know my customers are inspired by beautiful tablescapes, so I mix my offerings with large subject matter boards like tablescapes since those generate the most followers. I find that giving customers ideas for how the products can be used and styled is very powerful."

Melanie has a board called "Blissful Bedding" where her monogrammed pillow shams are interspersed with dozens of images of beautiful beds and bedrooms. She filled the "Bridal Shower and Wedding Gift Ideas" board with products that complement her own items, and she even pins press clippings about Luxury Monograms to add a level of authenticity.

So how does Pinterest fit into Melanie's overall marketing strategy? "For me, the real advantage of Pinterest comes from adding the Pin It! button below product images and blog posts—this encourages others to generate exposure *for* me. I have noticed that reminding people and making it easy for them to pin my products is the most effective use of Pinterest for my business."

Melanie has also hosted a number of successful contests through Pinterest. Contests further encourage fans to repin her products, gaining even wider exposure for Luxury Monograms.

"My followers are women who love to decorate and entertain. I develop effective information on my Pinterest account that inspires and educates on product usage and ideas. Inspiration is a very effective marketing tool."

Melanie, who now hosts webinars teaching other entrepreneurs how to use Pinterest, says the platform has shown her the real power of social sharing, and it has allowed her to find a new passion: "Each morning I wake up to an inbox full of stores wanting to carry my line, magazine editors wanting to feature me, and tons and tons of sales. The only thing I love more than seeing my business do well is being able to help other entrepreneurs do the same."

Pinterest contests are growing in popularity as a fun way for brands to inspire fans and promote products. HP hosts an ongoing Pinterest contest to promote its HP SpectreXT laptop. Each week the company announces a different theme on its website for fans to create a Pinterest board around. The board needs to include just one pin of the HP SpectreXT laptop, and entrants submit the Internet address for their board through the dedicated HP web page. Each week's winner is decided by public vote from the submissions, which are rewarded with prizes, including an HP SpectreXT laptop and $500 Amazon gift cards. HP has cleverly assimilated the contest into its own website, helping to drive traffic between the two and simultaneously collecting contact details from entrants. As the contest is ongoing, HP ensures that consumer engagement remains high and doesn't drop off after a single competition. By asking entrants to pin one image of the laptop, the company is promoting the product more widely, as there is a steady stream of new images of the product being added by a number of fans over time.[28]

Pinterest contests don't just have to be consumer focused—B2B companies can run successful contests too. Emailvision, a company that creates "software as a service" (SaaS) marketing solutions to deliver and automate e-mail marketing, ran a Pinterest campaign that targeted e-mail marketers and was designed to promote Emailvision's services *and* celebrate e-mail marketers at the same time. The "Pin Your Inbox" contest asked e-mail marketers to pin their favorite e-mail campaign to enter, and the prize was an e-mail creative designed by the Emailvision studio. The contest was smart—it focused on Emailvision's target customers, and so it raised awareness of the company's business, but because it encouraged e-mail marketers to send in beautiful campaigns, it was incredibly positive and generated a good vibe. Plus, the prize was one that the entrants would be happy to win.[29]

Intel is another example of a B2B brand that didn't shy away from Pinterest. With boards like "Tech Infographics," "Technology and Art," and "Geek Chic," Intel definitely owns its inner geek and shows its passion for technology (http://www.pinterest.com/intel). One of our favorites is the board called "Fan Love." Well, okay, full disclosure: Ekaterina was the one who created that board as part of Intel's Pinterest strategy in 2012. But what is fantastic about boards like this one is that it gives voice to Intel's fans. A combination of images from Intel fans from around the world and images created through the crowdsourced contest, the board truly shows what Intel means to those who love the company and share passion for technology. A word of caution though: make sure you have the right to use the image before you post it on Pinterest. Intel has gotten the artist's permission for every image posted on Intel's "Fan Love" board.

Pinterest is all about creativity. Its users are creative, and successful brands are innovative with ideas for boards and pins. The best brands on Pinterest are the ones that keep content fresh and topical, that

are dedicated to representing their brand in the best way they can to Pinterest's users, and that think about what they can provide that appeals to the interests and tastes of pinners. Pinterest is fun, slick, imaginative, artistic, and social. If your brand can be all these things, then you could find new audiences for your brand.

YouTube

Since its inception in 2005, YouTube has revolutionized the way we interact with video content. Advertising success can now be measured in viral YouTube hits, and video content has become seamlessly integrated with brand marketing in a way that was unimaginable before YouTube's online dominance.

One of the most important considerations for marketers is that YouTube is owned by Google, so make the most of search engine optimization (SEO) by choosing the right key words, titles, and video descriptions. By doing so, you'll enlist the world's largest search engine to help your content—and your brand—be discovered. Because of the power of Google behind YouTube, YouTube is the world's second largest search engine after Google.[30]

A recent YouTube redesign (called "One Channel") for brand channels means that you can have an intelligent banner image that will resize to look the same across all platforms, with the ability to embed social media links within it. You can also create your own 30-second video trailer at the top of the page to build your subscriber base. You can make more decisions over how your video lists are displayed and order them by related channels, interest lists, and content playlists in order to make the most of your content.

According to YouTube, optimized One Channel pages have driven a 20% increase of page views since they were introduced.[31]

Video annotations have revolutionized the way that marketers use YouTube. You can incorporate hyperlinks into the video itself to create

YouTube Facts and Figures

- YouTube is the world's second largest search engine after Google.[32]
- According to the Kelsey Group, of the 59% of those who viewed a video ad on the Internet, 43% went on to check out the company's website.[33]
- Streaming video delivers nearly three times higher brand awareness and message association and more than 100% higher purchase intent and online ad awareness than non-rich media ads.[34]
- The average YouTube user spends 900 seconds per day viewing videos.[35]
- 44% of YouTube's users are between 12 and 34 years old.[36]
- Over 829,000 videos are uploaded per day.[37]
- There are an astounding 3 billion views on YouTube daily.[38]
- More than 1 billion unique users visit YouTube each month.[39]
- 70% of YouTube traffic comes from outside the United States.[40]
- 72 hours of video are uploaded to YouTube every minute.[41]
- YouTube is localized in 53 countries and across 61 languages.[42]
- The average video duration is 2 minutes 46 seconds.[43]
- 25% of global YouTube views come from mobile devices.[44]
- Mobile makes up more than 25% of YouTube's global watch time, more than 1 billion views a day.[45]
- In 2011, YouTube had more than 1 trillion views or around 140 views for every person on Earth.[46]

a "clickable" interactive video. This opens up all kinds of possibilities to brands—viewers can follow the cue to click and find out more about a particular product, or you can put together an interactive commercial, during which users decide which outcome they prefer. You can use YouTube's metrics to find out the click-through of different options to learn about your customers' choices.

Marketers can also impose restrictions on viewers such as age or location. Brand channels can be featured on any website, and they are not limited to YouTube only, so they can become part of your main website, which can be a great option for SEO and viewers' discovery of your main company website.

YouTube can enhance a brand's global position in a way that could take millions of dollars in a standard advertising budget, and it can help a brand connect with hard-to-reach groups, such as 16- to 25-year-olds. A successful television commercial that goes viral on YouTube, such as VW's *The Force* (http://www.youtube.com/watch?v=R55e-uHQna0) or Evian's *Baby and Me* (http://www.youtube.com/watch?v=pfxB5ut-KTs), could expect to get tens of millions of views worldwide.

Since YouTube's launch, many brands have been quick to explore the marketing potential of video content from video blogging to educational videos, conference talks, and new advertisements. Successful brands mix in a variety of content on their *brand channel* to maximize customer engagement and show their audience different aspects of their business.

When you are setting up and managing your YouTube content, it's worth keeping in mind your marketing strategy: just what are you trying to achieve with this material? If you are trying to drive traffic to your website, make sure you include prominent links on your video's description as well as on your channel's home page. You can add banners or text to a video to give a call to action or remind viewers of your mailing list or a promotion.

You can use YouTube like a kind of video catalog, which cuts out the steps between more traditional advertising and purchasing. There is a growing trend among millennials in particular to use video to make purchasing decisions. By embedding ads in the video content, you can encourage viewers to click straight through to your store and purchase through the video.

Video content specialist Adjust Your Set created a series of click-to-buy videos for lastminute.com's YouTube channel, launched in the run-up to the holiday season.

STATS

Consumers who are in the 18- to 34-year-old age bracket are twice as likely to use video to determine which company to purchase from, and 38% are likely to visit a store that sells the apparel item after watching a video, while 34% of apparel shoppers are more likely to purchase an item after viewing an online video ad, compared to 16% who did so after watching an ad on television.[47]

The "Gifts for Him" and "Gifts for Her" videos ran for 10 days, and they attracted 22,682 views; there were 2,609 buy clicks on the gifts, with an average click-through rate of 11.5%.

A lastminute.com spokesperson said, "Video content like this where the viewer can click and buy products or services from us while the video is playing has proven that it drives sales and engagement for the brand, and we'll continue to invest in this in the coming year."[48]

In 2012, a video promoting a razor blade business called Dollar Shave Club went viral—and to date it has had over 10 million views on YouTube (http://www.youtube.com/user/DollarShaveClub). The video features the company's founder, Michael Dubin, walking through a warehouse giving essentially a stand-up comedy routine and telling men to buy his razors. The initial results were spectacular: the company's server crashed within an hour of the video going live from all the referral traffic as 12,000 orders arrived in the first 48 hours. The video launched the company and turned it into an overnight success.[49]

YouTube offers you a chance to be responsive to your audience. The in-depth analytics let you see not only popularity, likes, and shares but also demographics. You can use this information to make decisions on future content. For example, if you discover that you are popular in one part of the world or with one age group, you may wish to use more material to appeal to these demographics. Alternatively, you could look at why you are less popular with other groups and focus on changing that.

YouTube offers a chance for a more informal look at your company beyond your traditional advertising. There are many ways of connecting with your customers and reaching new audiences, so don't limit yourself to posting only your company's TV commercials—try and think of all the ways to use video to show a 360-degree view of your company and products.

> Video allows you to show a more relaxed or human side to your brand.

TIPS *for Engaging on YouTube*

- Add value and entertain. People come to YouTube to be entertained. They don't want sales pitches.
- There are options to add your social media links to the channel, but consider first if doing so will distract viewers from your featured link. Alternatively, if you are using content to connect and engage with your clients, you can make them aware of other places they can interact with you and remind people to like or share your content.
- If you are more focused on customer support and informational videos, be sure to use your video description and channel page to point to places customers can obtain more information.
- Think carefully about the length of your videos. The average video duration is 2 minutes 46 seconds, so if it is much more than that, there is a chance you could lose viewers' interest. Avoid putting too much information in one video: if it is too long, you could consider breaking it down into several videos covering separate topics.

- Consider posting videos in response to questions or comments from fans—it's so much more engaging than an e-mail.
- Keep track of statistics, and use them to inform your YouTube strategy.
- Mix up your formats with tutorials, behind-the-scenes videos, regular commercials, and extended versions of the story you are telling on traditional media.
- It's worth remembering your potentially global reach when it comes to searching for videos. Try to optimize your content and key words accordingly.
- Video is one of the most flexible and in-depth ways to tell a story, so get creative and use your imagination.
- Don't always get stuck on high-quality production. Sometimes videos shot on the fly with your phone or small camera that are relevant and will help engage your audience in real time are more valuable and more authentic.
- It's not all about you. Let your fans and customers tell their stories.

Your videos don't have to be limited to what you produce as a brand. You can let customers tell their own stories for a rich tapestry of real-life ways in which your brand has made a difference in their lives. Target recently created a commercial from home videos of real students opening their college acceptance letters (http://www.youtube.com/watch?v=NyD XdHVw-yM). The use of real people telling real stories in a powerful, visual medium meant that the campaign resonated with people all over the country. The campaign enabled a megacompany—Target—to build a personal relationship with its customers through visual storytelling.

Video can take the form of a conversation between brands and their customers. When consumers create a video (either to highlight your product or criticize it), it is a perfect opportunity to engage in the conversation and either thank them or turn them around or highlight some of the best features of your product.

In either case, your quick response might attract more traffic and create more conversations than the original video itself, as well as offer you an opportunity for creating yet another advocate. But you have to be agile and open to being creative and innovative in the way you provide your response. Much more on that in Chapter 5.

One great example would be Tiger Woods's video game. When a customer found a glitch in the game in which Tiger walks on water, he posted the video on YouTube describing the glitch and saying that no matter how good Tiger is, he can't walk on water. Tiger responded by posting a video in which the golf ball lands on a lily pad in the middle of the lake . . . and Tiger walks out on water, swings, takes the shot, and lands it right in the hole. The message read: "It's not a glitch. He's just that good." It's worth a watch: http://www.youtube.com/watch?v=FZ1st1Vw2kY. The video has had over 6 million views. Absolutely brilliant marketing! Agile and innovative responses connect with the customers on an emotional level.

Just before Christmas 2012, Ekaterina had her own encounter with the "wow" experience when her casual tweet to REI, "What is the best gift suggestion you have this year?" was answered through a video. Not only was the video custom made for Ekaterina, it was made within 30 minutes.

Even for the most innovative companies, that speed of response is to be envied.

Someone actually took time to create a custom response. Not only that, REI presented itself as a socially savvy brand. That piqued Ekaterina's interest, and she decided to meet REI's social media team and investigate further.

REI started its social programs about five years ago. The social team is composed of three people, all passionate about working with customers. It was a natural fit for the brand because the company is a member-owned co-op. "Our members are the source of our inspiration," said Lulu Gephart, social media team member at REI. "We love to bring our members' outdoor inspiration and expertise to life on our social platforms."

And it shows. One holiday season, the team decided to spice it up and answer holiday questions on Twitter with video. The program was called #giftpicks. To accomplish that, they used Green Vests—the in-store employees who pride themselves on their passion and expertise in various product lines and who are always available to help. Ekaterina's video response came from Charis, a Green Vest who works in the Bellingham, Washington, store.

The team shot about 90 custom videos during the period of several days. During that time the referral traffic to REI's site doubled. That is what we call "making marketing personal." Brands that embrace the personal touch and creative agile response through rich media and visual marketing are reaping the benefits.

One of the first company videos to go viral and make a real difference to that company's sales was made by Tom Dickson, who owns Blendtec, a company that manufactures food blenders in the United States. Back in 2006, he started making a series of videos, called *Will It Blend?*, shot in the style of tongue-in-cheek infomercials that simply showed him using Blendtec food blenders to blend ordinary household objects, including iPhones, credit cards, and golf balls. The videos went viral very quickly, and fans started writing in with requests for items to be blended, to which Dickson often responded (http://www.youtube.com/user/Blendtec).

The original video, featuring a bag of marbles being reduced to dust by Blendtec's hardy blender, has now been seen over 6 million times, while a video showing an iPad meeting its match has had nearly 16 million views. The channel has over half a million subscribers, with 130 videos now uploaded, and counting. Dickson likes to bring out themed versions for holidays such as Thanksgiving (blending a Thankgiving turkey dinner, naturally), and a World Cup version where he blends a vuvuzela (a plastic horn used in football matches in South Africa).

The popularity of the brand's series is staggering, but the impact on sales has been similarly impressive. Since the first video went viral in 2006, Blendtec has seen sales jump by over 700%.[50]

So what is the secret to Blendtec's success? There are several reasons why the *Will It Blend?* series made such an impression on viewers—and on sales. The format is brilliantly simple: everyone can relate to the corny infomercial style. And it's got that edge of misbehaving to it—we know our moms would never, ever let us blend half a dozen lighters (for good reason as it turns out: Blendtec had to deploy a fire extinguisher when the lighters exploded).

Tom Dickson is also really good at listening to fans and responding to their suggestions for items to blend, which has secured his popularity with followers. Dickson has also taken onboard that first rule of Internet content marketing: keep content fresh. New videos are always being released, keeping the product firmly in the minds of the hundreds of thousands of YouTube subscribers. Then there are the themed versions, inspired by holidays and events like anticipated product releases (the iPhone videos are some of the most popular) that keep the videos topical and add humor. The *Will It Blend?* series has now gained a total of almost 300 million views, and it has become an Internet meme in its own right. Not bad for a small blender company from Orem, Utah.

YouTube is a marketer's dream: it can connect with a global audience and show more dimensions to your brand than the more traditional made-for-TV commercials. The best brand YouTube channels use a variety of formats to engage with their followers, from the more traditional advertising videos to behind-the-scenes footage, meetings with team members, videos shot by fans, how-to or troubleshooting guides, or minidocumentaries about issues surrounding the products. As smartphone and tablet usage increases and becomes more a part of the everyday lives of people around the world, YouTube will become part of a forward-thinking brand's strategy to connect with audiences in ways unimaginable only a few years ago.

Facebook

One social networking platform has become significant in the lives of so many people that it has spawned a major Hollywood film, and its name has even become a verb. Have you Facebooked lately?

Since its creation nine years ago, Facebook has become a habit of life for many of its 1 billion users. It isn't "just" a social network: it has revolutionized the way we connect online. Facebook has opened up a global world to us from the comfort of our own armchairs, bringing people and organizations together in a way that has quickly become second nature but was unthinkable only a few years ago.

Facebook allowed brands and organizations to set up their own public pages in 2007, and ever since forward-thinking marketers have been using them—and the many improvements introduced over the years—to connect with their customers in ever more inventive ways.

One of the greatest assets of a company Facebook page is that text, image, and video posts can all be seamlessly integrated in a user-friendly design that encourages comments, likes, and shares from followers. Promotions and campaigns can go viral very quickly, and feedback from fans can allow you to generate two-way conversations with followers.

Visual posts really stand out on a company page and generate more engagement than text posts alone. Facebook is even starting to replace brand websites as a fan's go-to place to find out more about the company:

a recent study shows that 50% of Facebook fans prefer brand pages to company websites.[51]

Facebook has helpful guides for companies who want to start their own Facebook page or who want to make an existing one more successful at meeting their goals. Their Facebook for Business page has step-by-step instructions for setting up your page and getting the most from it. The page has a dos-and-don'ts section for choosing your cover photo, and Facebook gives tips for posting, such as these:

- Posts between 100 and 250 characters get about 60% more likes, comments, and shares.
- Photo albums, pictures, and videos get 180%, 120%, and 100% more engagement, respectively.

Facebook also tells you how to set up Facebook Adverts and Sponsored Stories to reach your target demographic, as well as how to monitor which adverts are more successful with the Adverts Manager function. There are tips for engaging your audience with relevant content and how to set up Facebook Offers to promote deals to your fans. You can promote your posts to reach more people, while Page Insights shows you what elements are working best and who is connected to your page. There are plenty of examples of best practices, such as "Post at least one to two times per week so that you stay top-of-mind and relevant to the people who like your page." Once your page is up and running, Facebook has plenty of advice on how to increase your influence and reach a wider audience, so be sure to check out their pages and read their helpful guides for businesses.

It is also worth taking note of how Facebook filters the content that appears in the News Feed. As mentioned earlier in the book, an algorithm called EdgeRank determines how much engagement your posts inspire and how interactive you are at responding, reading, and liking other people's posts. The more engaged you are, and the more engagement your posts receive, the higher your EdgeRank score, and your posts will be placed in a more prominent position in the News Feeds of your fans.

Facebook Facts and Figures

- A post that includes an album or picture receives 120 to 180% more engagement from fans than a text-based post.[52]
- Just 1 month after the introduction of Facebook Timeline for brands, visual content—photos and videos—saw a 65% increase in engagement.[53]
- Facebook users uploaded a record 1.1 billion photos during the 48 hours over New Year's Eve and Day 2012, nearly double the 300 million photos uploaded to Facebook on an average day.[54]
- 77% of B2C companies and 43% of B2B companies acquired customers from Facebook.[55]
- 80% of social media users prefer to connect with brands through Facebook.[56]
- More than 1 million websites have integrated with Facebook in various ways.[57]
- 74% of all marketers say Facebook is important to their lead-generation strategies.[58]

- 52% of all marketers found a customer via Facebook in 2013.[59]
- 85% of fans of brands on Facebook recommend brands to others, compared to 60% of average users.[60]
- Facebook is available in more than 70 languages. Internationally, Facebook ranks in the top two websites in every market except China.[61]
- Facebook accounts for 1 in every 7 minutes spent online around the world and 3 in every 4 social networking minutes.[62]
- U.S. desktop users spend an average of around 6 hours every month on Facebook; mobile users spent an average of 11 hours.[63]
- There are 2.5 billion content shares a day on Facebook.[64]
- There are 2.7 billion likes a day on Facebook.[65]

Marketers are beginning to realize the power of Facebook to connect with fans and to spread the word on new products and promotions. They are using it not only to reach out to new customers but also to turn them into loyal followers of a brand.

But how can a social networking site inspire this sense of potential for companies? Exactly how do you make the leap from friends' sharing photos of vacations, drunken nights out, and funny pets to empowering brands to drive sales through Facebook campaigns?

It is unusual now for a company not to have a Facebook page—there are presently more than 15 million brand pages on Facebook[66]—but there is a huge range in the way that companies are using the network. While some are happy to post the same content in a blanket way across their social media sites and link to their made-for-TV adverts, others are really getting behind the unique properties of Facebook to create communities and use it as a spearhead for marketing campaigns—with impressive results.

Facebook's recent brand page redesign focuses more on visuals, with "headline" photos taking center stage and larger images appearing on the Timelines. This is all great news for marketers. Out of all the various social networking sites, Facebook is still one of the leaders for community building and interaction with fans—and visual media are a large part of its success.

A 2012 study by ROI Research found that when users engage with friends on social media sites, it's the pictures they took that are enjoyed the most. Forty-four percent of respondents are more likely to engage with brands if they post pictures than if they post any other type of media.[67] It is especially true on Facebook.

Designer paper and analog brand Moleskine has harnessed the power of visual media to create one of the world's most active, prolific, and creative online communities. The company's visual content strategy focuses on user-generated content: it creates large-scale projects that users participate in by posting their own images and videos. Moleskine sales have risen 26% since 2006 thanks to a combination of imaginative marketing strategies.[68]

TIPS *for Engaging on Facebook*

- Don't just use generic marketing photos on Facebook. Create photos specifically to generate a conversation.
- Think how you can communicate visually—fans are more likely to comment on, like, and share a photo.
- Ask your fans to upload their own photos to give their perspective on how your products fit into their lives.
- Create campaigns specifically for Facebook that fans can join in with.
- Both photos and video work really well on Facebook and generate interaction with your fans.
- Get creative with your header photo, and choose something eye-catching and inspiring. Change it every now and then to keep it fresh.

- Integrate your regular marketing into Facebook, but let Facebook take it further. For example, show behind-the-scenes shots, or let fans decide what happens next.
- Global brands can make use of regional pages to target information based on locality to fans in different countries. Consider cultural differences when you design images or videos for a particular region.
- Don't worry too much about using professional photographs—a photo taken on a smartphone by a fan can sometimes tell a better story than a professional marketing shoot.
- Offer creative visual contests to engage your fans in a sustainable way.

A popular Moleskine Facebook campaign called What's in Your Bag? had users upload pictures of the contents of their bags into a Facebook album. The project generated thousands of likes and comments as readers looked at the contents of other bags (which included Moleskine notebooks, naturally) and shared photos with their friends.

Fans also post photos of themselves recommending their favorite Moleskine designs and showing how they use their Moleskine products on the Facebook page, which has over 170,000 likes (https://www.facebook

.com/moleskine). The company organizes events for enthusiasts around the globe, promoted through its Facebook page. Inspiring fans to create and spread images, customize the Moleskine notebooks, organize online competitions, and otherwise engage with the brand on a creative level has set Moleskine apart in its highly specialized market.

Successful companies often use traditional media and social networking to support each other, rather than choosing one or the other to focus on. In March 2011, the digital media company Neworld wrapped up a campaign for Irish organic dairy food producer Glenisk called the Tune Challenge, which used audio tracks submitted by fans on Facebook to find the soundtrack for their next TV commercial. The company says that "Glenisk experienced a sales uplift of 35% while the TV ad was on air. This is in comparison to when the ad was originally run in early 2010, at that time experiencing no significant uplift in sales. This integrated approach clearly delivered tangible results for the brand, much more so than just a television advert alone."

Glenisk reported the following results:

- There was a sales uplift of 35% when the ad aired.
- The company got national airtime on *Today FM*, plus national and local PR coverage to a value in excess of €200,000.
- There were more than 25,000 YouTube online views for the TV ad.
- The number of Facebook fans doubled.
- New fans, who joined for the contest, were encouraged to become customers through free yogurt coupons.[69]

Facebook has recently updated its services to offer brands customized regional pages based on where fans are logging in from. Some content may be the same around the globe, but companies can use the facility to personalize the experience depending on where their fans live, which has helped many brands better connect with their audience. The Harlem Globetrotters basketball team increased traffic coming to its website from Facebook by 230% with a regionally targeted social media campaign, which enabled the team to automatically serve unique content, such as regional game schedules, to its Facebook fans around the world.[70]

When it comes to marketing through Facebook, it is important to think carefully about the visuals of your page. Marketing software company HubSpot wanted to promote its brand on Facebook as a thought leader in the business-to-business field in an effort to increase engagement with fans and customers and to generate more leads.

HubSpot chose to feature a vibrant city landscape as its cover photo, as well as its company logo. The company developed a tab called "Try HubSpot!" in its main page view, allowing people to use HubSpot for free for a 30-day trial or request a demo to see how HubSpot can work for their business. In addition, it ran Facebook ads and used a strong call to action in its ads to encourage people to like its page (https://www.facebook.com/hubspot).

The company tested ads by targeting different age segments, including 24 to 34, 35 to 44, and 45 to 44, along with likes and interests. Eye-catching images were used to grab people's attention, such as the word "Attend!" along with information in the ad text about HubSpot's marketing conferences.

To increase engagement, HubSpot posted updates every day about marketing conferences and e-commerce tips as well as links to demos and videos, and it asked questions such as "Is mobile marketing a part of your strategy?" frequently to spark conversation among fans.

HubSpot also offered links to live chats with marketing experts from within the company on specific topics, and it ran Sponsored Stories to get the word out about its brand.

This mix of techniques, including a strong emphasis on visuals, led to some impressive results:

- A sales increase of 71% from Facebook users over the course of the 3-month campaign
- An increase in ROI of 15% from Facebook over the course of the campaign

- An increase of 39% in traffic coming from Facebook over the course of the campaign

Dan Slagen, head of paid lead generation, HubSpot, said: "We've found that actively participating on Facebook has engendered a valuable, open line of dialogue between HubSpot and its interest base. We're able to announce product updates, new e-books, and webinars, get feedback directly from customers, and gain inspiration for new ideas around inbound marketing all while generating new leads and customers."[71]

Intel is another company that puts emphasis on social engagement. Facebook is at the center of that strategy. The company's global page boasts over 22 million fans (https://www.facebook.com/Intel), with over 34 million fans in over 50 countries collectively.

Intel's strategy with social communications is about making its audience smarter while entertaining them. A lot of Intel's Facebook posts talk to the power of the "inner geek," something Intel's audience strongly relates to. An example of this strategy comes to life in the post seen on the right: "Avocados contain important mono-unsaturated fats that improve blood flow throughout the brain. Eating one is like going from a 56K modem to a high-speed ethernet!"

In a similar post, Intel educates fans on one of the company's core product's benefits—the light weight of an Ultrabook. Rather than showing the product specs or comparing it to something ordinary, Intel weaves an interesting fact about an obscure insect, a rhino beetle, into its marketing copy. This way, Intel is not only educating its fans about the product but it is also giving them interesting trivia in an entertaining visual. The post said: "The Rhinoceros Beetle can lift up to 100 times its own weight. That means it could carry 8 Ultrabooks on its back." Intel thus took a straightforward fact and made it instantly engaging and shareable.

Facebook has allowed companies to use their brand pages to improve customer service, talk to fans, encourage feedback, share images, drive sales, expand their marketing horizons, and encourage user-generated content. Followers are able to relate to brands as never before and to feel like they are an active part of the product experience, rather than a passive consumer.

Twitter

Twitter has broken out of its early stereotype in recent years as a microblogging site that appealed mainly to young people and techies, to become an innovative marketing tool for brands keen to connect with their audience and create a new kind of customer service

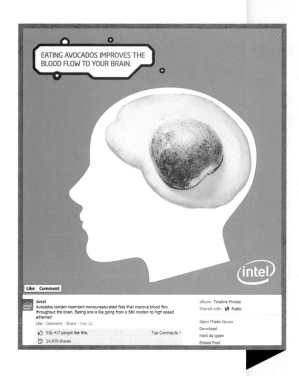

STATS

Twitter Facts and Figures

- More than one-third of all links shared on Twitter are images.[72]
- 67% of Asia-Pacific companies have Twitter accounts, showing a dramatic rise from only 40% in 2010; follower numbers quadrupled in the same time.[73]
- 83% of European companies now have Twitter accounts, up from 71% in 2010; follower numbers more than tripled.[74]
- U.S. companies with Twitter accounts remained at 72% (no change from 2010), but the number of followers per account more than doubled.[75]
- FG100 companies use Twitter in a variety of ways: to provide company news and updates (88%), to provide customer service (40%), to offer deals (28%), and to release career and job information (10%).[76]
- Over 460,000 accounts are created every day.[77]

- 20.6 million U.S. adults access Twitter at least once a month.[78]
- 177 million Tweets are sent every day.[79]
- There was a 182% increase in mobile account usage between 2010 and 2011.[80]
- 24% of users check Twitter at least once a day.[81]
- 54% of Twitter users are male, and 46% are female.[82]
- 46% of users are aged 18 to 34.[83]
- 42% of users utilize the platform to discover more information about a product or service.[84]
- 67% of users are more likely to buy products from brands they follow on Twitter.[85]
- Companies that use Twitter gain twice the number of leads each month than their non-tweeting counterparts.[86]

experience. Of all the social media platforms, Twitter is currently the most popular with Fortune Global (FG) 100 companies.

Recent redesigns have helped to create a more usable and visual layout. The simplicity of the format allows videos and photos to be viewed from within Twitter. Individual Tweets can now be embedded directly into websites or blogs and even responded to, creating new ways of interacting with followers. Users have far more interactivity than before, but without the clutter; this is a "clean" experience. Twitter also has an array of new keyboard shortcuts, which will appeal to marketers who spend a lot of time using Twitter.

The network has grown rapidly in recent years to embrace large new demographics, including companies and business users. The high percentage of young people on Twitter is just one of the factors that appeals to marketers keen to engage with this previously hard to reach group.

STATS

A recent study that analyzed 739,000 tweets found that 76% of content that was shared on Twitter had a photo attached, and 18% had a video as part of the message.[87]

Although primarily a microblogging site, Twitter has steadily been getting more visual. In 2011, Twitter added a new gallery feature that gave an image-based look to the network. This means that pictures now stay around much longer—100 photos can be displayed at any one time, so rather than disappearing down your feed, followers will be able to see all the images you've tweeted recently. It's worth sharing plenty of visual content or your gallery will look a bit empty. As these pictures stay around for a while, think about what you are tweeting and how the overall picture will look to an observer: Do you have a good mix of images, or do you tend to concentrate on one type?

Twitter cards are a recent addition to the site, and they have added a whole new visual dimension to tweets that make them far more engaging. Twitter cards make it possible for you to attach media experiences to tweets that link to your content. They are little summaries of web pages, such as articles, blog posts, products, or companies. Tweets that link to participating websites can be expanded by users to show a whole range of media, including content previews, images, and videos. It's worthwhile for marketers to be aware of the technology behind Twitter cards: if you add the code on your own site, you can determine what sort of content will be shown by a Twitter link. The potential for highlighting particular content could be very beneficial for visual campaigns.

There's a new twist to the Twitter cards too: lead generation. With this simple but brilliantly interactive tool, users interested in a particular offer or promotion will be able to fill out a field on the card that links to their existing information, allowing them to quickly register interest. This eliminates tedious steps in persuading followers to come to your site to register their details, and it integrates the website and Twitter experience in a seamless and slick visual manner.

There have been some imaginative ways to use the visual side of Twitter to run some recent marketing campaigns. Volkswagen Brazil used the fast-paced buzz of the social media site to create a storm of excitement around the country's largest—and sold-out—music festival, the Planeta Terra Festival in São Paulo, which was sponsored by Volkswagen to promote its new cool car, the Fox. Volkswagen hid tickets around the city and pinpointed their location on a microsite using Google Maps. The catch was that the map was zoomed all the way out—and the only way to make it zoom in to show where the tickets were hidden was to tweet the hashtag #foxatplanetaterra. The more times the hashtag was tweeted, the more the map would zoom in. For four days, fans raced around the city to get to the ticket giveaway locations, and the campaign hashtag stayed the number one trending topic in Brazil the whole time. What a creative blend of all the strongest features of Twitter![88]

Diet Coke wanted to promote women's heart health as part of its relationship with health organization the Heart Truth. The company held a contest in which people were asked to tweet or Instagram photos that showed something heart shaped using the official hashtag #ShowYourHeart. Coca-Cola pledged to donate $1 to the Heart Truth for every photo shared through February 7, 2013, and five winners were invited to the Red Dress Collection Fashion Show held by the Heart Truth in New York City. Thousands of people entered, generating awareness for the cause and for Diet Coke's association with the Heart Truth, and thousands of dollars were raised to help heart health. This inventive and altruistic campaign worked because it inspired people to think about the heart motif in a holistic sense: how the heart shape and heart health are part of their own lives. It created positive associations in people's minds about the Coca-Cola brand and its work with good causes, and all through a simple visual message.[89]

TIPS *for Engaging on Twitter*

- Have a strategy: don't clutter it with different messages. Develop your voice, and tweet around several key passion points. What do you want your followers to know you for? Why would they follow you?
- Use Promoted Tweet or Trend features to support your key messages. Photos and videos add interest, but they should integrate with the overall strategy.
- Keep material fresh by posting regularly.
- This isn't your company website. You can have a bit of fun with your images or graphics and show a more relaxed side to your brand. People come to Twitter to find interesting content.
- Many people won't visit your actual brand page. They will be viewing your tweets from their own stream or from a third-party application, so don't assume that your customers or clients will be able to see your previous tweets. Each tweet should therefore be able to be understood on its own.
- Mix up your content. Don't post the same types of tweets all the time.
- Ask questions of your customers. How are they using your product this season, or what feature would they like to see added?
- Use links. Link to articles, photos, or videos.
- Retweet. Find out what your followers are interested in, and share it with them.
- Use hashtags. Join in bigger conversations on a topic or start one of your own.
- Use calls to action. If you want something to be retweeted, say so. People are more likely to share your content if you ask them to share or retweet.
- Consider the location of the people in your audience. If they are mostly in the United States within the Eastern Standard Time zone, tweet your critical messages then. If you have a worldwide audience, maybe it makes sense to repeat some of your tweets during different times of the day when your followers will be most likely able to see them.

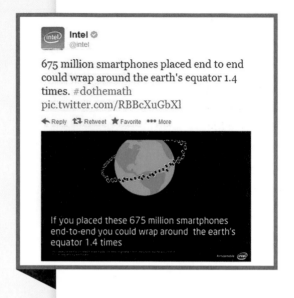

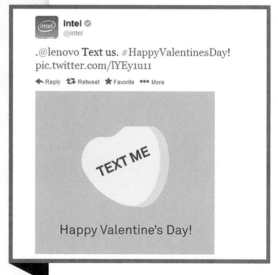

RadioShack used the Promoted Trend function on Twitter to ask people to upload a picture of themselves stretching out their hand, along with the hashtag #ifihadsuperpowers and a tweet of what they would do with superpowers, for the chance to win a mystery prize. RadioShack then digitally added a superhero costume to the photo and tweeted the photo back to the users! Several of the photos were randomly selected to win prizes from the store or RadioShack gift certificates. Due to the success rate and impressive increase in fans and positive sentiment, RadioShack's 2010 holiday campaign was selected from more than 200 entrants for the Forrester Groundswell Awards that year, winning top honors for its category "Business-to-Consumer North America: Energizing."[90]

In 2013 Intel began using the hashtag #dothemath on Twitter, and it's been the company's most successful hashtag to date. Intel includes a staggering fact or comparison, the hashtag, and an image. This really works well because Intel's followers like to have their minds blown by geeky statistics, and it draws them into the conversation. Intel has found that Tweets with numbers, statistics, and top-10 lists are generally recipes for success.

Another great example of interactive Twitter engagement is a Valentine's Day dialogue between Intel and Lenovo. Intel sent some of their partners custom Valentine's Day image tweets. Lenovo was one of the first ones to respond.

Intel said: *"@lenovo Text us. #HappyValentinesDay!"*

Lenovo jumped right in with this reply and a picture of the flowers made out of tech gadgets: *"@intel We got you these. Don't even need to put them in water."*

To which Intel responded with: *"@lenovo Awww . . . we're blushing! Thanks for the Valentine's Day love."*

Banter like this shows the brand's human side, its creativity, and its willingness to engage its partners and customers in the real-time dialogue.

Twitter has features that set it apart from other social media networks: it can generate buzz very quickly thanks to the trending element and the Promoted Trends and Tweets facilities, and individuals and organizations can have millions of fans so tweets can go viral almost instantly if they are picked up by influential figures. Using hashtags is a well-known method of getting your promotion out there to your fans and followers, but combining it with an image can encourage people to get creative and get the most out of this fast-moving network.

Instagram

The photo sharing newcomer Instagram is changing the way we interact with images and with the brands that post them. Although it is primarily a mobile-based app, this hasn't halted its spectacular growth since it launched in October 2010: it currently has 130 million monthly active users. Instagram photos (which are characteristically square, with artistic digital filters applied to them) can be viewed through Instagram or shared through sites such as Facebook (which owns it) or Twitter. Instagram relies on users' posting hashtags with their images, which allows people to discover related images or search for something very specific. But the hashtags also work through other supporting sites like Twitter to make it a social network that stands alone or that integrates seamlessly into other platforms.

Now that Instagram has added the ability to record and share video directly from the platform to social media, the feature is already beating Vine[91] in the battle to attract the biggest brands. The fact that Instagram is already heavily used by brands will help its new video feature be adopted quickly by companies looking for new ways to market products and connect with their followers. According to Mashable, videos shared by brands on Instagram have twice the level of engagement as Instagram photos and significantly higher engagement than videos on Vine.[92]

The features that make Instagram unique are these:

- There are 13 filters available to choose from to add mood and atmosphere to your video.
- You can add a static cover shot that serves as a thumbnail and/or title page.
- Recording time is 15 seconds versus Vine's 6-second clips.
- Users can record multiple clips in succession.
- There is a stabilizer feature to smooth out shakiness and make the product more polished and professional.
- The usual Instagram tagging works the same as with photos.

The Instagram app gives a new, creative edge to snapping photos or videos from a phone. The whole process of taking a photo, choosing a filter or digital effects, and uploading it online is slick and fun: Instagram is an app for the click-and-share generation. Although there is no equivalent to the EdgeRank filter or promoted content, the most liked photos and videos do make it to the popular page, and now that Facebook has integrated it into its service, media liked on Instagram shows up on the Facebook Timeline, helping to share images more widely.

Since brands started to have real success using image sharing networks such as Pinterest, social visual marketing has become more and more central to a company's strategy. Brands' quick adoption of Instagram shows how attuned they have become to telling their stories through visual media—and with 100 million monthly users, they really can't afford to miss the opportunities to reach new, young, vibrant audiences.

Like Pinterest, Instagram's user base is dominated by women, and as we know, women are responsible for the majority of household spending. Smart brands are consequently prioritizing finding new ways to grow online communities that will reach this target market.

Instagram Facts and Figures

- 67% of top brands are now using Instagram.[93]
- Instagram has more than 150 million users[94] with 100 million monthly active.[95]
- Instagram saw a remarkable growth in the first 7 months of 2012—going from 15 million users in early 2012 to 80 million in July—an increase of over 400% in just 7 months.[96]
- The Instagram network's user base is nearly 70% female.[97]
- Instagram leaders are luxury brands with Burberry, Tiffany, and Gucci among the brands with highest number of followers.[98]
- Users post 40 million photos per day with upward of 8,500 likes and 1,000 comments per second.[99]
- More brands are not only opening an account in Instagram but they are also posting upward of 20 or more times per month.[100]
- More than 5 million photos are uploaded to Instagram every day.[101]
- In 2012, Instagram users liked 78 million photos.[102]

Because of Instagram's instant, on the go appeal, companies are using it to humanize their brands, with plenty of behind-the-scenes and more informal content, as well as encouraging user-generated content, with great success.

The best-suited brands for Instagram are obviously the ones that lend themselves easily to images: luxury brands, retail, lifestyle, and fashion and design companies are natural fits for the platform. Your organization doesn't have to fall neatly into one of these categories to build a following on Instagram though. Intel is using it to show the creative side of technology with some beautiful, artistic images that have captured their followers' imaginations (http://instagram.com/intel).

American Express has similarly built on the opportunities that its product provides by posting lifestyle photos and the experiences that the product can enable, as well as shots of life at American Express HQ (http://instagram.com/americanexpress). The company has a vibrant community of over 27,000 followers, despite its being far from the typical Instagram brand user.[103]

Some of the most popular brands on Instagram are the ones who appeal to a younger demographic, such as Victoria's Secret, Starbucks, Forever 21, and MTV. Marketers have been working for years to connect with this key millennial age bracket, and visual marketing on Instagram can be a core plank to a successful marketing strategy.

With more than 2.2 million followers, Nike is an example of a brand that got behind what Instagram is all about, and it is using it to its fullest (http://instagram.com/nike). You may think that there are only so many pictures of sneakers and apparel you could post, but Nike uses the platform to tell a lifestyle story filled with everyday and extraordinary athletic feats. From running to playing soccer, tennis, snowboarding, and more, Nike mixes in iconic images of professional athletes with inspirational photos, prompting its community members to share their stories of athleticism and pride in living an active lifestyle. Nike also celebrates its community by hosting fan-generated images on Instagram. To do this, Nike encourages fans to use hashtags such as #makeitcount or #justdoit for a chance to have their photos shared with the larger community. Nike also looks for opportunities to commemorate on Instagram its own milestones with its community. For example, when Nike hit 6 million uses of the hashtag #nike on Instagram, the company spent 24 hours sharing images from the community that prompted them to "push harder." At the end of the 24-hour celebration, Nike ended by calling out the very first photo and fan who tagged #nike on Instagram, acknowledging that it takes both inspirational imagery and a passionate community to #makeitcount on the platform.

Instagram works well when it is mixed in with a brand's wider conversation with its fans. Clothing company Free People uses customers as models by asking them to use Instagram to post photos of themselves wearing their favorite Free People fashion. Those photos are then added to the website so that customers can see how the products look in real life, in a variety of styles. People can add comments and likes, and the company can build up whole conversations around the looks that fans create. The company has over 800,000 followers on Instagram (http://instagram.com/freepeople).

The brands that are already using Instagram have been quick to test out the new video function. The 15-second recording facility will be a relief to companies who have struggled with Vine's 6-second time limit, and it opens up greater possibilities for marketing ideas that need a little more space than Vine currently provides. Of course, having the mighty weight of Facebook's billion users behind the sharing potential of Instagram will help to persuade brands new to Instagram to explore its new function.

The filtering capacity that has made its photos so instantly recognizable will be of great interest to brands wishing to use the video feature for creative marketing. Its users have already been delighted with how easy the photo filters are to use, so the potential for producing artistic video clips and then uploading them straight to followers will surely be hugely popular.

Brands have certainly been quick to upload their creative video offerings. Burberry has been a keen Instagram user, with an impressive following of almost 1 million people (http://instagram.com/burberry). The Burberry Instagram video debut took us into the world of its Prorsum Menswear Spring/Summer 2014 show in London. The video gives the viewers a sense of anticipation of the show, with a subtle soundtrack and vintage feel. It is well shot and beautifully edited—and it has been well received by fans, who have heaped praise on it like these comments: "This is BEAUTIFUL. I wish I were there. " And "This video is inspiring!" Burberry is clearly an early master of the art of the 15-second Instagram video.

Lululemon's *Every Mat Has a Story to Tell* video shows what is possible in 15 seconds with great editing. This wonderful sequence splices together a yoga routine shot in different locations to create a smooth progression with changing backgrounds, showing how the company's exercise mats can be used anywhere. This video works as a slick but fun piece of marketing.

Charity:Water's take on the format captures in 15 seconds the difference the charity is able to make in people's lives. The video shows a woman called Sarpan Gamanga, who "often used to spend four hours every day walking to get water from a nearby stream." The 15-second clip is used to show the length of time it now takes to fill a container and walk to her house since the charity was able to supply water facilities by her home. By shooting the video in real time, the charity cleverly made the point of how quickly (within 15 seconds) the villagers can now access their clean water supply.

Instagram's unique features give brands the power to think creatively when it comes to marketing. Some of the most innovative campaigns of the last couple of years have included the use of Instagram—and they have redefined how we think of marketing.

On October 14, 2012, skydiver Felix Baumgartner successfully jumped 127,900 feet from space, and he became the first person to break the sound barrier without vehicular power on his descent. The stunt was sponsored by Red Bull, and the YouTube video has now been seen over 34 million times, surely the most extreme stunt ever performed—and the coolest product tie-in. Red Bull created a 360-degree social media campaign around the event, and its use of Instagram captured people's imaginations with Red Bull's step-by-step capture of the preparation leading up to the feat.

Red Bull posted 3,800 pictures in the run-up to the jump, giving fans an insider's-eye view as it happened. Red Bull's creative use of Instagram has earned it over 800,000 followers (http://instagram.com/redbull).[104]

The seamless link from Instagram to Facebook has been the inspiration behind some smart and imaginative recent campaigns that have benefited not only from the sheer size of Facebook but also the artistic, youthful edge of Instagram.

Ford's new Fiesta model is sleek and modern, and it appeals to a younger audience—just like Instagram. Ford harnessed the power of the Instagram-Facebook relationship to create a Europe-wide campaign

TIPS *for Engaging on Instagram*

- Build a community by putting your official hashtag in your banner heading for fans to know how to tag you.
- Show the human side of your brand by mixing behind-the-scenes shots with customer, employee, and producer photos and videos.
- Design and lifestyle are a big part of Instagram, so think how your product works in people's lives.
- Use filters creatively.
- You can find out more about your Instagram activity through their built-in statistics, so use them to inform your content as your profile evolves.
- Don't be "salesy" or use blatant product placement. Users of Instagram are media savvy, and they don't appreciate the community being used as a commercial.
- Brands that are popular on Instagram are original and artistic, and they blend their use of Instagram into their wider community building.

- Post regularly, and use the platform to show your take on current events, holidays, and seasons.
- Use specific hashtags for promotions or campaigns (which may or may not include your brand name). Using something like #HolidayPromotion is too generic—people will pick it up and use it with unrelated posts. Think carefully about hashtags, and pick ones that don't have a double meaning or that can be read differently, causing confusion.
- Don't use too many hashtags. Keep it simple; otherwise, your community will splinter, and there won't be a central focus to your brand's message.
- If people are posting comments, then make sure you join in the discussion and interact with your fans.
- Blend Instagram with your website for a more interactive experience. Instead of simply using your own product pictures, ask customers to upload their own photos or videos of how they use your product.

based on the Fiesta's stylish features. Each week people were encouraged to submit photos tagged with #Fiestagram and the latest feature-inspired hashtag such as #entry or #music, and a wide interpretation of the word was encouraged. The best photos were shown on live digital billboards across Europe as well as in online galleries, and the very best even won prizes, including a brand-new Ford Fiesta as the top prize.

The campaign particularly focused on the car's state-of-the-art features to raise awareness of the high-tech aspects of the car—something that would appeal to a new, younger, fashion-conscious audience—and to change perceptions of the traditional views of the Fiesta, which was already one of the most popular and recognized cars in Europe. Instagram's users (young, stylish, tech aware) were the ideal target audience for Ford's campaign, and the community building and sharing features of Instagram, coupled with the popularity of Facebook (the promotion was hosted on the official Ford Fiesta Facebook page), were perfect for the campaign.

More than 16,000 photos were submitted to the contest, and Ford's Facebook community gained 120,000 new fans during the six-week campaign, with hundreds of thousands of visitors coming to the galleries to view the submissions. Each day, the "popular" page of Instagram featured photos from the contest, raising awareness of the new Fiesta across the Instagram community of Ford's target demographic.[105]

Mashable points to Instagram's strong network of superusers, called Instagramers, as being vital to the campaign's success. When it came time to promote Fiestagrams, Ford knew that engaging this community would be key. So the company reached out to Gonzalez, founder of

Instagramers, and he quickly spread awareness of the contest to a broad audience. "We have groups throughout Europe—England, Germany, Italy, Spain, France, and beyond," said Gonzalez. "It's easy to promote a contest when you have 20,000+ followers on your side."[106]

In order to engage fans leading up to race day, the Indy 500 partnered with Seen to build an experience that allowed fans to share their Indy 500 journies (http://www.indy500orbust .com). By uploading photos to Twitter or Instagram and using the hashtag #Indy500orBust, fans were entered for a chance to win the ultimate Indy 500 experience. Unlike most hashtag-driven campaigns, however, #Indy500orBust didn't end there. For the first time ever, Instagram photos were incorporated throughout the Indy 500 marketing campaign, including an interactive map featuring geo-tagged photos (http://www .indy500orbust.com/map).

Fans shared 10,828 photos using the hashtag #Indy500orBust during the campaign's run from January 2013 to Memorial Day 2013. This number grew by 8,000 throughout the duration of the official race weekend, with a total photo reach of 53,162,862. The Indy 500 also gained 4,400 new Instagram and Twitter fans during that time.

One thing marketers might not realize about Instagram is its ability to test and try out visual content. Dunkin' Donuts has a passionate

cross-functional social media team that is always coming up with fun and creative ideas for visuals. Inspired by their office, which is affectionately known as "The DD Mothership," the team seeks out and tests everyday content moments on Instagram that are best captured in real time. Offering a behind-the-scenes look, photos of monthly sampling events where employees try new menu items and recipes being whipped up in the test kitchen are often shared as photos or videos on Instagram (http://instagram.com/dunkindonuts).

The team also looks for opportunities to weave in attributes of the brand's office culture, such as a passion for pink and orange Dunkin' Donuts nail art, or the internal "Tie Tuesday" movement, in which some employees proudly sport ties for fun. If a photo or video performs well on Instagram, the team may also consider it for use across other social media channels as a way to visually tell the story of Dunkin' Donuts' fun-loving and down-to-earth personality.

Instagram has a niche following—at the moment. Like Pinterest, as it grows, its appeal will surely broaden. Reaching out to a young audience of people with an interest in style, fashion, and technology is a core goal for many brands, and marketers can work with its slick, integrated features to create imaginative, innovative campaigns that stretch the boundaries of traditional advertising and appeal to new audiences around the globe. With opportunities like this, companies will want to make Instagram central to their visual marketing effort.

Tumblr

Tumblr is a blogging platform with a difference: it allows users to quickly reblog posts (text, images, video, quotes, links, or music) by other users with a click of a button. A Tumblr account is simple to set up, and it is visually appealing. And it plugs your business into a platform of millions of users searching for the best in visual inspiration. Importantly for marketers, Tumblr appeals to millennials and users with high levels of disposable incomes—both target demographics for brands. Tumblr was recently purchased by Yahoo! for $1.1 billion, showing that the platform doesn't just have the confidence of its millions of users but of the business community as well.

The key to Tumblr is its simplicity. Tumblr isn't about long blog posts and information-loaded content. Instead, it's for quick visual inspiration and consumer lust. Photos, videos, charts, quotes, and Q&As fill Tumblr streams, with users' reposting everything that catches their eye, wherever they are. It is fast paced, creative, irreverent, and entertaining—and it has street cred, often vital to brands hoping to attract younger customers.

One of the great features about Tumblr is that users can add comments only if they reblog your post, which cuts out a lot of comment moderating time for marketers, who would normally have to filter out trolling comments. This really helps the sense of community on the platform and gives it a positivity that can be lacking on other networks.

Tumblr has found favor with fashion companies and college students. Vanessa Gabriel's shopping website aSociete.com is one company reaping the benefits. aSociete offers exclusive discounts on top fashion brands to college students, offering as much as 50 to 80% off retail. Vanessa partnered up with other Tumblr bloggers, and as they started writing about aSociete, the signups started to come in: "It started to happen organically where random people on Tumblr would post about aSociete and how much they love us. Over 5,000 people came in off one organic post. It is crazy how viral pictures can go on Tumblr if they're trendy and fashionable at that moment."[107]

Tumblr Facts and Figures

- 50% of posts on Tumblr are photos.[108]
- An average Tumblr user spends 1 hour and 38 minutes on the site per month doing nothing but consuming content.[109]
- The average time per visit on Tumblr is 34 minutes.[110]
- Tumblr's unique visitors worldwide number is 117 million, which is up from about 58 million in 2012.[111]
- There are currently 113 million Tumblr blogs.[112]
- The total number of Tumblr posts to date is 52.3 billion.[113]
- 52% of Tumblr visitors are male.[114]
- 46.5% of Tumblr visitors are 18 to 34 years old.[115]
- 35.2% of Tumblr visitors have a household income greater than $100,000.[116]
- 48% of users have a college education.[117]
- 13% of Internet users 18 to 29 years old blog on Tumblr.[118]
- A recent survey by Garry Tan of Y Combinator found that Tumblr is more popular with 13- to 25-year-olds than Facebook, of whom 59% said they were regular users of Tumblr, compared with 54% for Facebook. Among those 13 to 18, the percentage who said they use Tumblr regularly was even higher: 61% versus 55%.[119]

Similar techniques work for other product-based companies. Sharon Gaffney cofounded MeebleMail, a company that transforms everyday e-mail into something special and unique with stylish personalized e-mail stationery. MeebleMail's demographic is women interested in style and design—so naturally, she wanted a visual medium to showcase her company.

So far, Tumblr has proven a successful marketing tool for MeebleMail: "Our main goal was getting the word out about MeebleMail and the e-mail stationery we offer. Tumblr has helped us from a visual standpoint, but it has also driven traffic directly to our website."[120]

"We are posting images of our e-mail stationery and other items from our design partners. We typically post images with very short captions," Sharon says, explaining that most Tumblr users prefer images that speak for themselves.

Sharon also points out that there's more to Tumblr than just posting images: "Like the other social media sites, Tumblr requires that you build relationships with other Tumblr users. You do this by tagging your posts so they show up in searches, following other Tumblr users, and reblogging relevant content. We use Tumblr as one of our social media tools in conjunction with Twitter and Facebook. I love Tumblr for the integration with Instagram and because it's visual."[121]

Even if your business isn't image or product based, Tumblr enables you to share images that relate to your demographic. Lindsay Lopez, professional Pilates instructor and owner of FORM Pilates—a boutique Pilates studio in New York City—uses Tumblr to offer advice and inspiration. Lindsay understands that her readers are into keeping fit and looking great, so she posts recipes, inspirational pictures, and quotes.

"So far, it's driven more people to my site, and I find that more people read it because it's so simple and visual as opposed to being a page full of text." Lindsay first stumbled across Tumblr after a fellow blogger suggested it as an alternative to a WordPress blog. Lindsay started early in 2013, and she is completely hooked: "What I love about Tumblr is that it is aesthetic. It's very visual, and it is easy to make a post look fabulous."[122]

As with any other social media platform, the keys to Tumblr success are post, promote, and participate in the community. Tumblr fills a niche by bringing together the best features of blogging and visual-based social media to create a unique platform.

The Tumblr crowd could be a perfect fit for many businesses. Vanessa Gabriel recommends companies try the platform and measure results to see if it works for them: "Tumblr is a great resource to promote your products and merchandise to thousands of people, increasing the sales and user base. I truly believe Tumblr is an untapped marketing gold mine that has yet to truly be capitalized by many companies. It's been awesome for us!"[123]

While IBM does not produce products that are directly suited to the Tumblr crowd, the company has built a successful presence as a content *curator*. The company shares business and technology information (videos, graphs, photos, infographics, and short posts), and it has built up a community called *A Smarter Planet* around their expertise (http://smarter planet.tumblr.com).

The World Bank has shown that you can have great success on Tumblr despite not falling into any of the traditional Tumblr categories. The organization's leadership team has been using social media for a few years as a way of sharing the World Bank's mission and message, but they wanted to use Tumblr specifically to give an interesting angle on what the World Bank does. The team set up to run the account made use of the very extensive data bank that the organization has collected over the years to post charts, along with short explanations, to visualize the fight against world poverty. The blog is clean and simple, with clear data that cleverly makes the best of the organization's role. The World Bank Data Vis Tumblr page (http://worldbank.tumblr.com) has received all kinds of positive attention online, and it has turned out to be a great success, according to social media strategist and site creator Liana Pistell. She made the wealth of data digestible and interesting, and the outreach to the Tumblr audience fit perfectly with the organization's wider strategies.[124]

It's essential to have a strong and simple theme to your Tumblr blog. Coca-Cola's theme Where Happiness Lives Online (http://coca-cola .tumblr.com) captures the message of the brand perfectly with photos, cartoons, quotes, GIFs, and video snippets that support Coca-Cola's message of happiness. The brand representative says: "Random bursts of Happiness and Positivity is the heart of Tumblr. That's why Coke's teen fans flock to it to share those expressions with each other, and that's why the brand belongs here. Wherever Happiness is being shared, Coke is bound to be there." The blog attracted over 12,000 visitors, 1,300 followers, and 300 notes and reblogs in the first six weeks since launching in December 2011, and it has fulfilled the purpose of a high level of teen engagement with a focus on positive content and community building.[125]

TIPS *for Engaging on Tumblr*

- Let pictures tell the story on your Tumblr account with text being secondary.
- The best times to post content, according to bit.ly, is between the hours of 7 p.m. and 10 p.m. EST on Monday through Thursday, not including just about any time on Sunday.[126]
- Use relevant tags so that your images show up in searches.
- Reblog plenty of content from other users.
- Relationships on Tumblr are important. Follow other users and comment on posts.
- Keep your target audience in mind, and repost content that is relevant to them.
- Keep a focus on your goals. Don't drown out your message by reposting everything and anything.
- Have a strategy and a calendar so you can keep up a steady stream of quality content.
- Keep in mind your brand identity, and don't post anything that could compromise that. There is plenty of humorous but inappropriate content on Tumblr so stay professional when representing your brand.
- Keep a good mix of product information, lifestyle posts, and other content around your brand so your feed doesn't appear too overly commercial.
- Combine visual, text, quotes, audio, and video in your feed.
- Stay consistent with your tags. Fans are more likely to use your tags on related posts if you have a handful of "official" tags that you use.
- Keep content fresh, and post often. Tumblr is a fast-paced platform.
- If your goal is to drive traffic to your website, keep an eye on your analytics to see what sort of posts drive the most traffic, but don't make the mistake of posting that content only in the future. Users like variety on Tumblr.
- If you are new to Tumblr, spend some time getting to know the platform and the kinds of content that people post.
- You can incorporate a Tumblr blog directly into your corporate website, which is great for search engine rankings (but make sure that blog content is suitable for your corporate image).
- You can use Tumblr as an overview of what's on your website. *Rolling Stone* magazine uses Tumblr to give photos and snippets of articles, and Tumblr visitors can then follow the links to the full features on the magazine's main site if they want to learn more.

BBC America's Tumblr feed for its show *Doctor Who* (http://doctorwho .tumblr.com) won the "Best Overall Brand on Tumblr" award at the industry's Shorty awards in 2012. The blog "drives tune-in for *Doctor Who*, BBC America's highest rated show ever, and it keeps fans active and engaged throughout the year." The blog gained 82,000 followers in just 10 months. The show's Tumblr uses with great success a mix of user-generated content, behind-the-scenes shots, program screen shots, GIFs, and images from real-world fan meet-ups in order to re-create the whole world around the show. It is a simple premise, but it gives richness to the fantasy universe the BBC has made, while taking it further. With an average of over 1,300 notes per entry, the Tumblr feed has captured what the platform is all about, and it is hugely popular with fans.[127]

Adidas has proved that Tumblr can fit into wider marketing campaigns with its successful Tumblr campaign in 2012. When Adidas bought its month-long campaign, it was one of the first brands to purchase advertising when Tumblr announced it would sell paid promotions on the site. The retailer created its soccer blog for the 2012 UEFA European Championship (http://adidasfootball.tumblr.com), being played across Poland and the Ukraine, and it planned to promote the site with paid placements in the Tumblr Radar slot on the user dashboard. The Adidas Tumblr features a YouTube video of football stars saying "Tumblr" in their native languages, as well as photos and animated GIFs. The site was a part of the wider marketing campaign around the tournament, and it aimed to build a large community of football fans. Adidas's global brand marketing director, football, Tom Ramsden, described his vision for the Adidas football blog: "We will use Tumblr to share unique content with fans; combining material from our vast footballing archive with fresh, new content produced in real time by a lineup of exciting, up-and-coming producers."[128]

The brand has continued to use Tumblr to support wider marketing and brand initiatives, such as the #mygirls campaign being aired in Russia, China, and Korea, which looks to explore the strong bonds between women in sport and to promote a healthy lifestyle for girls.

If your brand wants to connect with teens, college kids, and young professionals, Tumblr is a great platform to find a new audience. Take time to get to know the platform before you start to post, and think hard about simplifying your brand message to get the most out of the platform's mix of visual content. Even if you don't have a brand that lends itself to your own visual content, many organizations have built a strong following curating other people's posts to build a community around their expertise.

Vine

Lately, the craze for Vine—the app that lets you post short, maximum 6-second video footage loops—has gotten brands thinking about how to use the tool to showcase products and expand their social media content. The app's popularity has been exceptional: within three months of its January 2013 launch, Vine had grown to be the top free app on iTunes.[129]

Vine is similar to Twitter (the company that owns it) and Instagram in that users share video clips on the social network, but the clips can also be embedded in Twitter and Facebook posts. Initially launched on Apple, Vine is now also available on Android, so expect its use to leap from its current number of 13 million users as more fans get hooked.[130]

The app makes it simple to record your clips simply by tapping your smartphone screen—the app only records while the screen is being pressed, so you can either record one continuous shot, or you can record using stop-motion filming to give a speeded-up effect and condense a longer event into the 6-second limit. Vine also records sound, so you have to think about the audio element of your videos as well.

People can like, comment on, and share your footage with other image sharing networks, so clips can go viral across networks. You can also tag your clips in the same way you would with Instagram photos and Tumblr posts.

Vine offers marketers as many ways of telling your brand's story as photos—and maybe more. What can you say in 6 seconds? The speed

STATS

Vine Facts and Figures

- Branded content accounts for 4% of the top 100 tracked Vines.[131]
- Branded Vines are 4 times more likely to be shared than branded online videos.[132]
- 5 Vine tweets are sent every second.[133]
- Most Vine activity occurs between 10 and 11 a.m. EDT.[134]

- Of the top 20 retweeted Vine videos of all time, only 1 is from a brand: it is the movie teaser from *The Wolverine*.[135]
- More Vine tweets occur during the weekend than all of the weekdays combined.[136]

at which brands jumped onto the platform shows how many are seeing opportunities for short videos to go further than photos alone. For the online retailer, Vine can offer a 360-degree view of a product that photos alone can't capture; for the creative marketer, a 6-second video could be a viral commercial; for the smart community building brand, the app is a way to reach out and connect with fans.

Within a short time of its launch, brands were already offering different examples of how short video clips could be used in the context of their brand. Lowe's home improvement store created a series of how-to videos with the hashtag #lowesfixinsix showing simple home improvement tips, life hacks, and ways to perform various tasks using stop-motion animation.[137]

MailChimp is an online mailing list company famed for its quirky monkey character who acts as the site's tutor and offers tips, tricks, and links to fun online distractions. With Vine, MailChimp has been able to take its trademark monkey character further by featuring him in videos that entertain as well as help raise awareness of the brand. The clips take MailChimp marketing to the next level while keeping the brand of humor and online memes (such as the company's monkey mascot and office dog Maddie standing on things) that their fans love and recognize.[138]

TIPS *for Engaging on Vine*

- Make sure your social media manager has full approval to use Vine because clips are posted instantly.
- It is best to approve content ideas in advance because you can't save drafts.
- Stop-motion videos are among the most popular for brands. They allow you to be creative with your footage by turning it into an animation or else shortening a sequence to highlight product features (for example, showcasing how a kitchen gadget works or how a piece of furniture is assembled).
- Vine is perfect for creating a short product showcase ahead of a launch. Taco Bell celebrated the release of its Cool Ranch Doritos Loco Taco with a Vine video, and it was rewarded with more than 2,500 retweets.[139]
- Instead of the 30-second or one-minute ad, think how you can convey your brand message in 6 seconds.
- Have fun with your ideas. Dove recently posted a clip of a bar of soap "ball" hitting shower gel bottle "pins" in a bowling game.[140]
- You can get behind the scenes at your company by posting fun footage—but make sure that everyone is aware of the filming before you start.

- Run a contest, and ask users to post their own video responses. Urban Outfitters launched a Vine contest with Converse in which fans were asked to post clips showing a day in the life of their Converses. Videos had to be tagged with #yourchucks, and the winner won items from both Urban Outfitters and Converse.[141]
- Tag your clips to ensure that they are found by people who are not following you directly.
- Keep it simple. Many people will be watching on smartphones, so don't try and make your clip too detailed or overly complicated.
- Don't rush your footage just to fit it into the timeframe. Think of it as a minicommercial.
- Think about the sound as well as the vision. If you are recording live footage, try to eliminate background noise, and/or consider using a backing track.
- You can essentially make animations using stop-motion shooting. Many brands have gotten creative with this idea to make beautiful or impossible things happen around their products.

You don't have to limit yourself to product showcases. How about showcasing a service? SweetShot Photography is a boutique photography company that used Vine to promote headshot sessions. They shot a short behind-the-scenes video of how they stage a headshot session, finishing with a shot of an empty stool all set up for you to join them for your own shoot. The next day, @sweetshotphoto tweeted that it had generated new leads thanks to the Vine post.[142]

Vine can also be used to host contests or sweepstakes, allowing brands to crowdsource unique content from their fans. As the temperatures increased during spring 2013, Dunkin' Donuts hosted the Running on #IceDD contest to celebrate the return of iced coffee season. The contest

prompted fans to use Vine with the hashtag #IceDD to show how Dunkin' Donuts iced coffee put a spring in their step for a chance to win a one-year supply of Dunkin' iced coffee. Five runners up also had the chance to win gift cards to Dunkin' Donuts. Throughout the promotion, Dunkin' Donuts also created three of its own #IceDD videos to raise awareness and inspire its community on Vine to participate. The contest ran for one week, and it generated a range of energetic, creative submissions. It's important to note that any video contest will offer a higher barrier to entry because it's more work to participate in than, say, text or photo contests. However, pursuing this path has the potential to generate much stronger, shareable content that can leave a lasting impression with fans.

The creativity and integration with Twitter continues to propel Vine into new arenas. Dunkin' Donuts also generated headlines for being the first brand to incorporate Vine into a professional broadcast: ESPN's *Monday Night Countdown*. Throughout the 16-game season, Dunkin'

Donuts created four Vines, each 5 seconds long, to replace the static on-air billboard within the program.

With the goal of bringing an innovative and interactive social media experience into one of America's favorite pastimes, Dunkin' Donuts also introduced the #DunkinReplay into *Monday Night Football*. Each week, with a team from Dunkin' Donuts and the Hill Holliday marketing agency on standby, the company produced a #DunkinReplay Vine, re-creating a marquee play from the first half of the *Monday Night Football* game using Dunkin' menu items. The Vines were created during halftime and tweeted in the fourth quarter in order to maximize the second screen experience and to make the brand a natural part of the conversation around *Monday Night Football*. Each #DunkinReplay Vine delivered as many impressions as a comparable TV spot (at significantly less cost).

It's fair to say that Vine's integration into other, larger platforms such as Twitter and Facebook is going to help its steep upward trajectory as more and more users download the app and enjoy the creativeness that it inspires. For brands, Vine offers yet another way to catch the attention of audiences across platforms in a busy social media environment. If you think of the 6-second opportunity in the same way you would think of a 30-second TV commercial, there's no reason why Vine can't be part of your visual marketing strategy and have as big an impact as any other campaign media. Vine encourages innovative, imaginative responses to the 6-second constraints, so start thinking what you could do in that time to reach out to your fans.

SlideShare

It's easy to overlook online presentation sharing website SlideShare as a platform for visual marketing, but it is an important business network: with 60 million monthly visitors and 130 million monthly page views, it is among the most visited 200 websites in the world.[143] Users upload presentations, webinars, Word and PDF files, tag them, and share them on

STATS

SlideShare Facts and Figures

- With 60 million monthly visitors and monthly 130 million page views, SlideShare is among the most visited 200 websites in the world. [144]
- SlideShare has 5 times more traffic from business owners than any other website.[145]
- SlideShare is heavily used by small business owners and microbusiness owners.[146]
- SlideShare's audience comes from a range of sources: organic searches, other social networks, and other SlideShare content.[147]
- The 5 most popular topics are business, technology, travel, education, and health.[148]

- The average number of slides per presentation is 19.[149]
- The 6 most-used tags on SlideShare are *business, market, trends, research, social media,* and *statistics.*[150]
- Popular presentations contain more images (37, on average) than other presentations (which contain 21).[151]
- SlideShare was recently voted to be among the world's top 10 tools for education and e-learning.[152]

SlideShare or other social media sites such as LinkedIn, or they embed the files in their blogs and company websites. SlideShare has also been referred to as "the world's largest professional content sharing community."[153]

Like LinkedIn (the company that owns the site), it is mainly used by the business community, and the two networks complement each other. SlideShare presentations can be uploaded into a LinkedIn profile to add an extra dimension of knowledge and expertise to your company or individual image. While the basic platform is free, there is a paid-for professional platform that allows you to brand your channel and have ad-free pages, and it gives you access to analytics.

When it comes to community building and lead generation, especially in the B2B sphere, SlideShare can demonstrate expertise in your field, and it works very successfully as visual content marketing. SlideShare isn't about quick fixes and viral memes, but about networking in a virtual space and having something in-depth but shareable to use to connect with colleagues and customers.

SlideShare isn't just about sending information outward. The social functions in the site are giving companies the potential to connect with customers and clients in new ways, generating new business and enhancing their online image.

SlideShare also allows you to amplify your message. If a webinar or conference presentation reached only a few thousand in its original format, SlideShare can have a multiplier effect once the presentation is posted online. Think back to Ekaterina's example of using a deck uploaded to SlideShare to promote her book *Think Like Zuck*. The presentation "12 Most Profound Quotes by Facebook's CEO Mark Zuckerberg" was viewed by more than 97,000 people with no paid promotion behind it.

Being innovative in technology use to get their message across can help organizations of all sizes connect with new audiences. Sharing presentations can show users a company's ethos far better than the more traditional LinkedIn, Twitter, and Facebook routes alone. In-depth presentations can make a company more three dimensional and add personality.

In May 2011 NASA launched its NASA Universe channel on SlideShare (http://www.slideshare.net/NASA), which integrated presentations, documents, and videos from their headquarters and field centers. In the announcement on the SlideShare blog, NASA Social Media Manager Stephanie Schierholz said: "NASA always is on the lookout for new ways we can engage people in their space exploration program. SlideShare provides us another great way to share our content in new ways and new places with the goal of inspiring and interesting people in the universe."[154]

An increasing number of companies are using SlideShare to present financial, technical, or other in-depth information that can be difficult to represent on their websites using more traditional tools such as graphs and text. SlideShare enables them to connect with potential clients in a whole new way. Pfizer uses SlideShare to post its financial reports, allowing interested parties to access that information in a user-friendly format (http://www.slideshare.net/pfizer).

SlideShare can be used for a variety of goals, with community building, demonstrating expertise, and content marketing among the most popular. SlideShare is particularly effective as a lead-generation tool. When the employee recognition software company Achievers wanted to drive more leads from HR executives, it developed a strategy that took three months to plan. By sharing strong content on social media, the company used SlideShare to help position itself as a thought leader in its field. The company launched five presentations specifically designed for the site, and it used SlideShare's ability to include a lead-generation form within the presentation. Achievers shared the presentations across its social networks and blogs, and within seven days of launch, it received so many qualified lead forms filled out by HR executives that the leads made up 77% of all incoming social media leads that week. The presentations got 42,000 views in the first seven days, and traffic from SlideShare to the Achievers website made up 30% of traffic from social media—beating out Facebook and LinkedIn referral traffic combined.[155]

With limited time for travel, SlideShare can be used to expand your global reach. Enterprise software company Salesforce.com had a goal of making its content more visible to a wider audience and create brand consistency of its wide variety of content.

Salesforce produces hundreds of presentation decks, tutorials, e-books, infographics, and white papers. "Previously, teams were setting up SlideShare accounts on their own," says Jennifer Burnham, director of social strategy and content marketing at Salesforce. "With this decentralized process, we didn't have a coordinated brand presence or a clear picture or pulse on what content the different teams were publishing." The company created a custom brand network on SlideShare to bring all of its content together into one place and drive more traffic to the main channel (http://www.slideshare.net/salesforce).

Advanced tools like private sharing have enhanced Salesforce's internal collaboration. Presentations, documents, and videos are uploaded

TIPS *for Engaging on SlideShare*

- Don't try to cram too much onto each slide.
- Don't use cheap-looking graphics or commonly available stock images.
- State the problem at the beginning of the presentation, and then give the solution.
- With presentations, less is often more. Give details of where people can come to learn more if they wish.
- Limit the length of the presentation. People may lose interest if it is too long.
- Embed the presentations in your company blog, and link to them from your social media accounts.
- Respond to comments to generate discussion and provide more information.
- Give your presentation a catchy, relevant title to grab people's attention.
- Make use of the tagging functions to help people find it. People often come across presentations when they are searching for something very specific, so think about the best tags to describe it.

- Don't make it a blatant commercial for a product. Be sure to give information that people will find useful.
- Think about using images or diagrams instead of words to convey a point. You can say much more on a slide this way.
- Use SlideShare to create an expert community: IBM has its own channel based on industry topics.
- SlideShare can make an easily digestible alternative to downloading your company reports.
- Use the analytics function to understand how people engaged with your presentation, and use that information to inform your visual content strategy.
- SlideShare is a great lead-generation tool. Use all of its lead-generation features to provide relevant calls to action at the end of the presentation.

and shared privately with teams for review. But the greatest benefit the company has seen with SlideShare, Jennifer says, is the "interaction and discoverability of content" with prospects, partners, and customers.

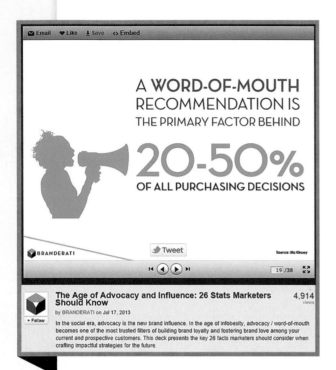

"With SlideShare, we're able to expand the reach of our best content to people who may not necessarily be familiar with our brand and people who may not be visiting our website or attending an event," says Jennifer. "In essence, by posting a deck to SlideShare, we are extending the reach and lifetime value of that content."

SlideShare's lead-generation features have helped Salesforce generate and assess the quality of hundreds of sales leads. The sales cloud team, for example, posted the *Social Sales Revolution: 7 Steps to Get Ahead* e-book on SlideShare and received 16,900 organic views and gathered more than 300 qualified sales leads. Salesforce CEO Marc Benioff's "Welcome to the Social Enterprise" keynote deck received more than 122,000 views on SlideShare—far more than it would have if it had been presented only live or posted on the Salesforce.com website.[156]

The right SlideShare content can be of huge value added to your niche audience. Slides with lists, quotes, statistics—any aggregation of valuable data or advice around a particular topic—do very well on the channel. For example, BRANDERATI, the company that provides advocacy and influencer marketing platforms and services (disclosure: Ekaterina is a cofounder and CMO), put together a slide deck that showcased a collection of statistics around advocacy and influencer marketing in a visually appealing way called "The Age of Advocacy and Influence: 26 Stats Marketers Should Know." The deck was organically viewed by over 5,000 people and provided numerous leads for the company (http://www .slideshare.net/Branderati).

If you are looking to use content marketing to expand your audience among business and industry professionals, then SlideShare offers a smart alternative to other networks. It gives you the built-in advantage of being able to share SlideShare content easily across platforms and promote it on other networks.

Google+

In November 2011, Google+ unveiled *brand pages*, enabling brands and businesses to use its social networking platform. Since Google is the world's favorite Internet search engine, its foray into social media has been snapped up by business owners eager to improve their SEO and keep up to date with social media trends.

For businesses, Google+ offers many advantages of other social networks, as well as including several unique ones. It has LinkedIn's business mentality: an open interface and networking strengths. It has the usability of Facebook and some of the news and interest aspects of Twitter. Its strengths lie in its openness, its community features, and its streaming facilities; it holds huge potential for brands keen to engage and connect with their audience and build new networks.

Many brands that have joined are still not showing true engagement; many just aren't sure what Google+ offers that Facebook doesn't. However, the recent increase in buzz surrounding the business opportunities is beginning to convince more technologically focused businesses in particular. It's not just the numbers of new users. It's who they are: tech-savvy, business-minded people who are looking to connect, share, and engage.

What hits you first about Google+ is the prominence of visuals in a profile page. The cover photos have recently been expanded to up to 2,120 by 1,192 pixels, so you can show off the visual side of your company to its best advantage. However, the cover photo dominates your profile to such an extent that you can be let down by a subpar photo. It's worth putting as much effort into choosing or commissioning an image as you would with any marketing campaign.

Its look is clean and well organized, but a real advantage of Google+ is Circles: the ability from the outset to separate your connections by interest or industry. For brands, the Circles feature adds new potential for interacting in different ways with customers, employees, colleagues, the media, and other businesses. News and updates can be shared with only the relevant audience, meaning that brands can engage very differently with colleagues and customers.

One of the best community functions about Google+ is the Hangouts. You can have private video chats with a select group of people—or you can broadcast the chats publicly or record them for marketing purposes. Recorded Hangouts are automatically posted to YouTube, helping them reach an even wider audience.

Rather than straight-up numbers and stats, Google+ has opted for a feature called Ripples, which is a graphic that shows how a post has inter-acted with other users, literally like a ripple effect. This is useful for seeing how far your information has spread and the sorts of interactions it has inspired.

Google's +1 feature is similar to Facebook's like button. The +1 fea-ture gives users a way of showing agreement or interest in content, and it allows them to share the content on their own stream if they wish.

Central to Google's vision for Google+ is the integration of Google+ data into the regular Google search engine. Google is the largest search engine in the world, and information shared on Google+ is prioritized in searches, which has huge implications for your SEO. Having a presence on Google+ is also important for businesses who have a local presence because their profile is automatically integrated into Google Maps, so people searching locally for businesses will be able to see more about you—which can give you the edge over your competitors.

Brittney Bogues, CEO of All In PR, a digital PR firm geared toward pro athletes and nonprofits, finds Google+ essential for her business. For her, it's the way the platform integrates with other Google tools that makes it

Google+ Facts and Figures

- There are now over 250 million Google+ accounts with 150 million active users across the globe.[157]
- Google+ has now overtaken Twitter as the world's second largest social network.[158]
- Google is the world's favorite search engine, with 80% of unique searchers.[159]
- People in the United States, India, and Brazil are the most active on the site.[160]
- Google+ users are likely to be students, developers, engineers, designers, and photographers.[161]
- A great majority (42%) of users are young adults, mostly 18 to 24.[162]
- Video is the second most posted content type on Google+, whereas on Facebook, video is less likely to be in the top 4 content post types.[163]
- Overall, the top brands on Google+ reflect there being a stronger male audience with traditional male brands doing well—for example, car brands, football clubs, pinups, gaming companies, and tech blogs.[164]

so much more than just a social networking site. "It helps with managing our calendars, networking internally and externally, and keeping us updated with current events. This allows us to add real time content to our clients' digital accounts as well as our own."

Yolanda Shoshana, the "Luscious Lifestyle Diva," runs a lifestyle company for women. She's a speaker, consultant, writer, and wedding officiant, and she uses her Google+ page primarily as a marketing tool. She says the platform has presented her with multiple business opportunities through networking with other professionals: "Through Google+, I have been recommended for writing gigs, and I've been invited on a few shows as an expert. I actually got a high paid column gig for six months because someone on Google+ had been following my work and recommended me."

And, of course, there's one key advantage to utilizing the social media platform of the world's biggest search engine. Ashli Norton, cofounder of SimpleLeap Software, the company behind Workitywork—an app that helps teams give kudos and manage their workday in a fun and interactive way—has found that Google+ has been integral to raising her company's profile online. "I've noticed links that I share in Google+ land in Google's search results much quicker than sharing them on our Facebook company page or on Twitter."

Quick indexing of links can be vital for businesses wanting to stay on the leading edge of their niche. It's no surprise that Google will be looking to its own social network first for the most up-to-date information.

Yolanda says she's had the most results using the Hangouts feature, which is a live video chat service unique to the platform. Google launched Hangouts On Air, which allows you to broadcast your Hangout video for anyone to watch. Yolanda is very excited to use this service: "With the addition of Hangouts On Air, I am going to revamp my online talk show to launch a lecture series and connect with my followers and fans."

Ashli has found Google Circles to be the best tool for networking for her business: "I love sharing specific news and posing questions to the groups. Plus, when it's time to make a contact—for instance, with someone who may be interested in something our business is doing—I go right to the circle I need and contact everyone who would be interested."

In the beginning, Brittney found the vast array of features available overwhelming, and she suggests that businesses begin by taking a Google+ tour: "It helps you to grasp the superb functionality of it and how it helps your business stay organized. You want your staff to be educated on all the different dynamics of Google+ and take full advantage of what it has to offer."

Just like any other social networking site, Google+ can help businesses get ahead if they're clever about how they use it. Brittney, Yolanda, and Ashli all stress the importance of sharing information and connecting with your community. "Nobody wants to hear all about your business and your business only," says Ashli. "Make sure for every business-related message, there are other interesting messages to follow. Keep it personal; keep it interesting."[165]

Photographer Trey Ratcliff has nearly 5.5 million followers on Google+. He has used his visual talent to take advantage of Google+'s ability to put images center stage and build up an impressive audience. He often has 2,500 or more +1s, and hundreds of people will share his posts, all because of his skill with visual social strategy.

Ratcliff's strategy can be used by marketers to build their own brand audiences:

- Try to tell a story through your images, and tag everyone involved or interested.
- Follow people whose posts and images you can share to inspire others. Ratcliff says, "I believe curating my own list of people to follow is very, very important. I need constant inspiration and ideas, so I circle up people who give me ideas, make me happy, and make me think."
- Host Hangouts, and share them on YouTube.
- Share your YouTube videos on Google+ to get cross-pollination between the two sites.
- Tell stories by sharing visuals of behind-the-scenes activity at your company. Or tell stories of customers and how your product has improved their lives. Add great captions to make the images stand on their own.
- Regularly point back to your website to let customers find out more. Ratcliff says, "I think of Google+ and these tools as leaving scent trails to a bigger food source, if you accept the superorganism communication analogy."[166]

Google+'s popularity with young, tech-aware people has made it the network of choice for brands eager to connect with this demographic.

Chocolate manufacturer and London 2012 Olympics sponsor Cadbury wanted to expand its audience among this very group, and the company decided to use some of the unique features of Google+ to build a community of the network's users (https://plus.google.com/+CadburyUK). The company's goals were to engage with the 18- to 25-year-old audience, stand out from other Olympic sponsors, and extend their reputation for creativity and innovation.

From the outset, Cadbury explored the potential of Google+ to the fullest. Cadbury shared exclusive and creative content that fans couldn't get anywhere else. For example, special edition Google+ chocolate bars were made to feature on the page, and Cadbury even sculpted a chocolate version of its Google+ page. "We've really tried to do things that are unique to Google+," says Jerry Daykin, social media community manager at Cadbury.

The company used Circles to target information at users with different interests—for example, sharing recipes, posting Olympic news, or collecting feedback from a Tasters' Circle.

The Cadbury team broadcast frequent Hangouts, giving fans the chance to interact with Olympic athletes and chocolate experts. By promoting its Hangouts, Cadbury grew its Google+ follower base by 150,000 people: "Hangouts are a really great way to quite literally see people eye to eye," Jay has observed. "At the end of the day, humans like communicating face-to-face, don't they? With social media we've kind of been reduced to just writing to one another; it's interesting to see people's faces again."

With the number of followers growing rapidly and a steady stream of exciting content, the Cadbury page was featured on the Hot on Google+ page, which further accelerated its followers.

The results were impressive:

- Increased the click-through rate across all of Cadbury's AdWords campaigns by 17%
- Added a consistent 10,000 new Google+ followers per day
- Increased the traffic from Google URLs by 7.5%
- Helped reach over 3 million total followers[167]

Cadbury has shown how to make the most of its Google+ profile, linking it to their wider marketing for events or product launches but tailoring content specifically for their Google+ audience.

TIPS *for Engaging on Google+*

- Google+ supports long posts, so you can combine more scholarly posts with shorter, snappier ones, along with photos and videos.
- Make the most of the Circles feature by sharing different content with different groups of people, so everyone gets information relevant to them.
- Remember that having an active profile can boost you up Google's search engine, so keep content fresh, and post regularly.
- Make the most of Hangouts by using them as promotional material. You can broadcast them to followers.
- When you are adding people to Circles, think hard about how you label them. Don't just add them all as "followers." You get the most out of Circles by being specific and then sharing targeted information with each group.

- Use the Events feature to promote future launches, conferences, meetings, presentations, or awards that your circles might be interested in. It sends out invitations that then sync with Google Calendars.
- You can use the Ripples feature to find out more about how your posts have been shared. If a few key individuals are influential in sharing your content particularly widely, you may wish to build a relationship with them to help your reach on social media.
- Use relevant key words and links in your About page to help drive SEO.
- Google+ has a powerful search facility, so use it to add businesses, colleagues, or people with similar interests to your Circles.
- Be sure to add the +1 feature to your company's web page or blog if you want the content to be shareable onto Google+.

Google+ has the power of Google's search engine behind it, so marketers would be wise to think about the SEO advantages of sharing information on their profiles if nothing else. But if you want to expand your audience among a young, tech-savvy crowd, then Google+ can be a great place to connect with them. The network is growing rapidly, so think about what its unique features can bring to your brand—and to your community—allowing you to take full advantage of your presence there.

Developing a Visual Storytelling Road Map: From Strategy to Implementation

If you're anything like us, brainstorming, strategy sessions, and content planning make our hearts beat a little faster—in a good way. It's such an exciting time to incorporate visual storytelling into your social media program and develop a strategic road map that will set you up for success in the long run.

Visual storytelling is more than just producing stunning images, videos, and other visuals. It's a way of thinking. In order to be successful, your visual storytelling program must have clearly defined goals that are in alignment with key business objectives. To achieve those goals,

> Tactics without a strategy is worse than doing nothing at all.[1]
>
> —**LI EVANS,** author of *Social Media Marketing: Engaging Strategies for Facebook, Twitter & Other Social Media*

companies need to take a hard look at how their current efforts compare to where they want to be in the future. Identifying strengths, weaknesses, and opportunities will help to determine what additional resources are needed to achieve these goals.

In addition to setting goals, content planning is key to strategically developing visuals that will bring your company's story to life. Planning for what you can control and developing a robust visual library will help your company to be more nimble when the unexpected happens. It will also allow you to focus more on content distribution and engagement, both of which are key performance indicators (KPIs) for visual storytelling success. In this chapter we'll offer tips and resources for measuring program success, and we'll show you how the right analytics can help you tweak your visual content strategy on the fly.

It's important to note that the step-by-step process and solutions shared in this chapter can be leveraged regardless of your resources or head count. We often hear, "Oh, but I'm a one-person department," or, "I'm a small business owner." Phooey! Passion, enthusiasm, and a can-do attitude are the very first things you need to embrace visual storytelling. Some of the best visual storytellers out there are small businesses because they live and breathe their story each and every day. We're here to offer thought starters and a defined process that will have you looking at and capturing the visual world around you a little differently.

Are you ready?

Setting Goals

There's no denying that social media can be a powerful tool, but too often companies get caught up in producing a stream of content, and they don't think about the big picture. Or worse, they get caught in a cycle of random requests from departments across the company who are all competing for space on the social media content calendar. Instead of perpetuating the cycle, align your visual storytelling strategy with your company's goals and vision for the future. Whether it's corporate, marketing, branding, or customer relationship management (CRM) goals, a visual storytelling strategy will resonate more with your target audience if it's shaped around key business objectives.

It's easy to think of this as limiting, but the reality is quite opposite. Having a clear understanding of the role visual storytelling can play in achieving your company's goals on social media is a creative catalyst. It will help you to define your vision and identify the components that will bring your visual story to life. It will help you identify the supporting themes, content buckets, visuals, and social media platforms at the heart of your strategy. And it will help you identify what success metrics to evaluate as you ramp up your visual storytelling program.

The key is to keep your goals reasonable. Select several goals that are the most important to your business and that are feasible to achieve through social media. Here are examples from leading companies regarding their visual storytelling goals:

- Awareness and education
- Branding
- Competitive differentiation
- Consumer engagement
- Corporate social responsibility
- Customer retention
- Fan and community growth
- Lead generation
- Loyalty
- Positive press
- Product launches
- Promotions
- Referral traffic
- Sales
- Thought leadership

A good example of the role goals play in developing a visual storytelling program can be found in Burberry's Art of the Trench Tumblr and website. Launched in 2009 and still an ongoing campaign, the sites are described as "A living document of the trench coat and the people who wear it."[2] Through the sites, Burberry targets current and aspirational trench coat owners, with its goals structured around raising awareness, referral traffic, sales, and branding.

Supporting themes of this story are told visually by the photos of the people featured, which include a range of men, women, and children. Each person has a different look and a unique way of styling his or her trench, allowing contributing themes of personal style, quality, universal appeal, and wearability to shine through.

By curating a visual storytelling experience, Burberry's customers rewarded the company with more than just awareness and a celebration of the trench lifestyle. Just one year after launching the Art of the Trench website (www.artofthetrench.com), it generated 7.5 million views from 150 countries, plus higher-than-average conversion rates from the click-throughs to the Burberry website.[3]

Auditing and Analyzing

Once you've defined the big-picture goals, it's important to understand how your current efforts stack up. Start by conducting a content audit of how your efforts are performing across all of your social media channels, and cross-reference it with the overall social media conversation about your company. While the word *audit* sounds daunting, we're going to make this process as easy as possible. It's important that you recognize how you're currently allocating your content, whether your content themes are in alignment with goals and key business objectives and what your content's strengths, weaknesses, and opportunities are.

Evaluating Your Current Efforts

If you already have a system for measuring your social media content efforts, that's great. If you don't, we recommend building a good old Excel spreadsheet.

The purpose of this process is to identify the ways in which your current social media content strategy supports your goals and to identify your top-performing content themes and types. The end goal is to evaluate your current program and create a benchmark against which to measure your visual storytelling efforts going forward.

We understand fully that some companies may just be starting out, while others have been incorporating visuals into their social media content calendars for some time. Whichever the case, this exercise will force you to evaluate all of your efforts by platform and dig a little deeper into the rationale behind the messages and content types you're putting out.

Determine a reasonable timeframe in which to run these metrics, with the schedule depending on your frequency of posting to social media and the tools and resources you have at your disposal. If you can build a larger sample size of three to six months, that's fantastic, but if two is more scalable, do the best you can.

Tracking Data

If you decide to do the audit yourself in a very basic way, in the Excel spreadsheet you want to look at key factors that play a role in the success of your content. Depending on your social media audience, posts may be more effective at specific times of day, or your fans may prefer photos to videos. To evaluate these factors, create a spreadsheet with a different tab for each social media platform you have a presence on. Keep each of the following as individual columns or rows so you can filter as needed.

- Date
- Time of day
- Day of the week
- Content type: for example, photo, video, text

- Content theme: for example, product, promotion, sale, thought leadership, funny
- Engagement metrics for the platform: each as a separate tab or row (for example, likes, comments, shares, retweets, click-throughs)
- Paid media support for the content: for example, dollar value
- Engagement rate per post
- Post sentiment: positive, negative, neutral
- Qualitative wins

For engagement rates of your posts, tweets, and so on, here are quick and easy ways to calculate them:

- **Facebook.** Look at the "virality" of your post in Facebook's page analytics. If you prefer to calculate yourself, this figure takes likes, comments, and shares and divides them by the total impressions generated per post.
- **Twitter.** Calculate a basic engagement rate with the number of replies and retweets divided by your number of followers that day multiplied by 100.
- And so on.

Qualitative wins could be inclusion in a news article, a response from an influencer, becoming a trending topic, or a surprise number of leads generated. These may be harder to remember the further you go back, but they're valuable to capture and record when you can because numbers won't always tell the full story.

Analyzing the Raw Data

Having this data in a spreadsheet will also allow you to filter by each factor and look at the raw data for trends or themes. Evaluating these supporting components, plus your content's engagement rate across all of your social media channels is one important step in pivoting to where you want to be going forward.

When looking at your social media content metrics, here are a few questions to ask yourself:

- What does my post frequency look like: for example, number per week and time of day?
- What does my content mix look like across text only, photos, videos, infographics, presentations, and more?
- What percentage of my posts by social media channel are visual?
- What topics do I post most frequently about?
- Am I posting the same content and creative across all of my platforms, or do I personalize content by platform?
- Do these topics align back with the key business objectives I want to support with social media?
- Are there any topics that I'm missing?
- Is my company's voice, personality, and corporate culture coming through in my posts?
- What social media platforms are currently performing the best and worst for my company?
- What are the characteristics of my top 5 to 10 posts across each social media platform?
- Am I supporting any posts with paid media? If so, what are the spend, frequency, and post types?
- Have there been any qualitative wins as a result of my company's social media content over the past year?

Listening to Customer Conversations and Sentiments

In addition to analyzing your proactive social media content efforts, you also need to listen to what your customers are saying about your company online. Studying your customer's frequently asked questions, overall sentiment, favored social media platforms, and their use of visuals is important for several reasons. First, it allows you to determine if your proactive content and what your consumers want to hear from you are in alignment. Second, social media conversation about your company is a powerful focus group. Understanding what your consumers' frequently asked questions are, plus what they gush or gripe about, will help to drive your visual content strategy. It can also help you prioritize what social media platforms you invest more time in and the types of visuals you use.

Here's what you should be listening for:

- Frequently asked questions
- Conversation topics
- Conversation sentiment: overall and by popular topics
- Conversation spikes by topic, time of day, and day of the week
- Favored social media platforms
- Frequently used visuals: for example, photos, videos

Arguably the best way to glean this information quickly is to invest in a tool like Radian 6, Sysomos, Social Mention, or others. But if you are on a tight budget, these can be a little spendy. If you don't have budget and resources for a social listening tool, you can do this the old-fashioned way. Analyze your social media platforms when you're conducting your content audit to gauge how responsive your fans were to each piece of content. For example, if you're on Facebook or Instagram, look closely at the comments. See if fans responded in line with the content topic, the sentiment of their comments. If their responses are largely off topic from your content, look closely for key themes.

You can also search for your company across all of the major social media platforms to take the temperature of the general chatter. Facebook may be challenging with privacy settings, but the introduction of hashtags may generate some interesting findings. Platforms like Twitter, Instagram, YouTube, Vine, Pinterest, Google+, and Tumblr are all very searchable. Learn what and how people are sharing—news articles, photos of their in-store experiences, reviews on a product or service, and more. Social listening tools rely on users with public account settings, which means you won't be able to get data from all of your customers, but it will serve as a good sample size.

Social media at its finest is a continuous, two-way dialogue between your company and your customers. If you can use social listening to inspire relevant content ideas that prompt conversation and engagement, you're one step further toward hitting those key objectives.

Summarizing Your Audit

Once you've gone through auditing your efforts and consumer conversations online, summarize your top 5 to 10 key takeaways. What really jumped out to you? Was it that posts on Monday morning always perform above average, or that your consumers take a ton of photos of your products? Do customers talk about one thing on Facebook but something completely different on Twitter? You may have even identified FAQs that are asked over and over again, or you discover an unexpected use for one of your products. All of these takeaways can be translated into themes for your content calendar.

Depending on your resources, it's good to go through this process on an ongoing basis. Even if it's not as robust, going through a topline process monthly with a deeper dive quarterly will help to keep you on track. It will also ensure that you're not missing any new themes or trends to craft content around. Just because your customers were saying something one month doesn't mean that it will carry on forever. The best companies and brands on social media strive to be nimble to change and tweak their content themes as needed.

It's not until we look closely at our efforts that we understand our strengths, weaknesses, and opportunities. Studying your current efforts and how your consumers perceive your company are key to your content planning and measurement efforts. It will also give you that much-needed support to turn down that completely off-topic, off-strategy post request the next time it crosses your desk.

When brands use data and historical analysis to optimize their engagement strategy, they see a significantly higher impact than they would see with just using random visuals.

> The BRANDERATI team found that using a data-optimized content strategy can increase brands' social engagement 2,000 to 4,000%. Using data-optimized visuals can increase brands' social engagement 40 to 60%.

Both Ekaterina and her strategy and account teams at BRANDERATI are huge believers in the data-optimized approach described above. Granted, they do use a proprietary analytics and engagement tool to answer the questions we raised above in a much faster fashion than any manual analysis could. And by doing so, they help a large list of their clients reach unprecedented levels of engagement on their social properties.

Running the data across a variety of brands and industries over the past two years, the BRANDERATI team found that utilizing a data-optimized content strategy increased their clients' engagement on their social media properties. Even brands with a significantly sized and established social media presence saw their monthly engagement increase with the use of historically optimized and strategically placed visuals versus the use of posts with randomly selected visuals.

One example of a brand that saw success with this strategy was DIRECTV. The company's content strategy includes a large variety of elements such as TV and celebrity news, movie, and sports updates, as well as a complete rundown of offers and features DIRECTV provides. It is critical for a brand with such a diverse content strategy to identify the most popular and relevant types of content to help drive the highest level of social engagement possible. Partnering with BRANDERATI, the team identified significant peaks in engagement around the brand's content over the summer of 2013. One of the things they found was that DIRECTV's Facebook engagement increased by 148% when they initiated social conversations about the TV series *Duck Dynasty*! Armed with this information, DIRECTV decided to create a larger three-tiered engagement program related to *Duck Dynasty*.

The first step was to develop weekly content schedules and increase the number of *Duck Dynasty* updates and features. The team designed and posted countdown images to the season premiere, which were wildly popular among their fans. The brand also used this information to boost their ongoing Facebook fan acquisition campaigns. The company targeted

Duck Dynasty fans in its outreach. This campaign allowed DIRECTV to acquire more fans with an increased propensity to engage with the kinds of content it were already posting, at a lower cost. In addition, DIRECTV partnered with the A&E network to launch a Facebook application game tied to the show. This game, called *Duck Dynasty* Quack Match, engaged fans and gave them an opportunity to enter a sweepstakes and win daily prizes. *This approach, along with using various similar visual tactics, led to an increase in monthly total engagement of 56% for the three months in the summer of 2013 over the previous six months.*

Social media analytics helped DIRECTV stimulate and grow its community of adoring fans by providing a clearer view of what their fans were passionate about. Utilizing results from social analytics to drive marketing initiatives outside of a social posting strategy is extremely important, and it can lead to success for a brand outside of its own digital ecosystem.

In developing and executing any social engagement strategy, it is important to know the people in your audience and what they like. It is crucial to study how your fans behave and react to different types of content, and apply those findings to future strategic plans.

Another example of a brand that used this strategy is the National Basketball Association (NBA). Leveraging lessons gleaned from previous engagement analysis, BRANDERATI's and NBA's marketing teams developed a creative social content strategy.

One series of posts implemented during the 2013 postseason that worked particularly well for the NBA was the We're Moving On posting campaign. So at the completion of each best-of-seven series, the team designed a post with an image of the winning team that accompanied by the message: "WE'RE MOVING ON TO THE [SEMIFINALS, FINALS, and so on]". Other strong performers for the brand were Facebook albums. So the team designed a series of albums filled with predictions for the results of each game series. For example, at the start of the Heat versus Spurs best-of-seven finals, the album posted included eight images, one for each potential result (Heat win in seven games, Spurs win in seven games, Heat win in six games, Spurs win in six games, and so on). Fans were encouraged to share the image that included their prediction for which team would win, and in how many games. Both of these campaigns created a consistent feel to the page and a repeatable success for the NBA.

In addition to these campaigns, the team wanted to create a few posts that would really stand out and create buzz. One idea was to design and post championship rings and banners for the Heat and the Spurs, countdown posts leading up to the crucial finals game 7, and even posts celebrating Father's Day and the NBA's Social Media Awards. And fans loved it! These posts even got picked up by *Bleacher Report, Fox Sports*, and the NESN channel. *This visual strategy and creative thinking led to an increase of nearly six times more shares than the previous year's posts.*

> Visual storytelling is the confluence of art and science, balancing an intended message with purpose and mutual value while investing in the medium and the culture that defines it. It's not only meant to be consumed but also designed to be shared . . . educating, informing, and entertaining along the way.
>
> **—BRIAN SOLIS**

Shaping Your Visual Story

Now starts the really exciting stage of taking your goals and current social media content efforts, plus any new learnings, and translating them into your visual storytelling program. A little planning goes a long way in terms of keeping your efforts strategic and on track.

Goals may be the backbone of your visual storytelling program, but translating them into a powerful story requires meaningful supporting content. Think of each piece of content you share as a visual vignette contributing to the larger story your company wants to communicate. Each piece of content needs to have a clear theme and point of view, much like a chapter or scene, plus a takeaway message for the reader. The content also needs to be aligned with who you are as a company in terms of voice, personality, and values. Once woven together, these themes will shape your visual story.

Themes can come from many places, so we recommend a little exercise that involves looking at how your goals, company voice, and customer feedback can be supported with visual content.

Start by listing out your goals and jot down very topline responses as to how visual content can help achieve them. Aim to have about three supporting points for each goal, but you can always grow the list as needed. If your goals differ by social media platform, then go through this process for each of them. Here's our sample:

XYZ Company Goals and Supporting Themes

1. Increase sales
   a. Raise awareness for products and services
   b. Communicate promotions, coupons, offers
   c. Target communications for new store openings or product availability
2. Promote brand differentiation
   a. Easy-to-find locations and long hours
   b. More variety of offerings and competitive prices
   c. Fast and friendly service
3. Grow customer loyalty
   a. Show customers how much we care about them
   b. Show role our products and services play in their life and lifestyle
   c. Communicate how we reward customers

Look closely at these goals and supporting themes, and they will likely be in line with key brand differentiators. Chances are, these themes are closely tied to message points in a company tagline, advertisements, mission statement, and more. If there's anything major missing that's a key company goal or brand differentiator, now is the time to add it.

Although a good start, this alone will not communicate a cohesive visual story. Next, look closely at your company's voice and personality. Social media platforms all require a more human touch than other online communications. This offers a good opportunity for your company's voice to shine in a relatable, personable way, allowing your customers to build a different type of relationship with you.

This may sound strange, but to bring out your company's voice, it helps to play a little what-if game. If your company were a person, what would it be like in real life? If you need help deciphering this, look at how you communicate to your customers on your website, in advertisements, e-mail communications, and your social media channels, and pull out the more human qualities. Remember, you want to embrace social media's more personable, human side. Breaking this out will identify other important visual content themes that bring your company's story to life.

XYZ Company Voice and Personality

1. Hardworking
   a. Commitment to quality
   b. Works hard to meet and keep customers
   c. Values customer feedback
2. Down to earth
   a. Easy to relate to
   b. Appeals to a wide audience
   c. No unnecessary frills
3. Fun to be around
   a. Likeable
   b. Shows you a good time
   c. Keeps coming up with new ways to have fun

Last, but certainly not least, it's also important to go back to those consumer insights you pulled from your customers online. Sometimes the person we want to be versus how others see us are two very different things. Visual storytelling can help your company to bridge those gaps and personify those key values to enhance your reputation. Make sure to call out personality traits that are strong versus weak so you can develop a plan on how to organically strengthen those values through visual content.

In addition to personality strengths and weaknesses, you also want to look for the most commonly discussed conversation themes from your consumers online. Make sure to call out if these conversational themes differ by platform because doing so will allow you to further personalize content themes to their most relevant audiences. Compile these themes and feedback with any supplemental information you can get from your marketing, market research, and/or your customer service teams and build those into common theme or topical buckets:

XYZ Company Customer Conversation Themes

1. Frequently compare and contrast product and service offerings
2. Most likely to shop at night after work
3. Love free samples and demos
4. Often comment on music played in the store
5. Mixed reviews on salespeople—some good, some bad

Are you starting to see themes and topics that you can craft visual content around? You should be. Based on XYZ Company's goals, personality, and customer feedback, it appears that its visual story should be shaped around its being a hardworking, down-to-earth, customer-centric company. Content themes should be crafted around how the company puts customers first and its key brand differentiation points and promotions. To play up the fun and down-to-earth elements, the company can develop lifestyle content showing how its products play a role in consumers' lives, and it can talk about the fun in-store elements like freebies and music playlists. To aid customers in reviewing product and service offerings, blog and video demos can be drafted. And to align with customers' shopping habits, most digital offers should be posted in the evenings.

By going through this process with XYZ Company, we've shown how you can shape your story and identify major themes to craft your visual content mix by looking at your goals, company voice, and customer feedback by social media platform. In the next section, we'll explain how to determine your visual content mix from topic, medium, and platform perspectives.

Determining Your Visual Content Mix

Successful visual storytellers understand that the magic is in the mix. Mixing up types of content and different media—from photos to videos, infographics, and more—keeps your visual storytelling fresh. It also allows you to deliver more personalized content to target audiences across different platforms with the ultimate goal of keeping your customers engaged and coming back for more.

For visual storytelling, it's important to personalize your strategy and content mix by platform. There will be opportunities for content to overlap and be used across multiple platforms, but this will be dictated largely by the platform best practices plus the customer insights and preferences that you uncovered through social listening.

> Publishing is now a Paris café. Sometimes you read the news; other times you pet the cute dog.
>
> **—JONAH PERETTI,** Founder and CEO of BuzzFeed[4]

The first step in determining your visual content mix is to evaluate your desired frequency per platform for posts, tweets, pins, and so on. For example, if you post 30 times per month on Facebook, you want to define how many of those posts will relate back to your most important and relevant visual storytelling themes. While the concept is simple enough, the challenge is that social media managers are faced with a never-ending stream of requests for space on the content calendar. Having a formula and clear plan will not only keep you organized but will also help you to educate colleagues the next time they want to "get something on Facebook."

In this section, we will share tips for determining your content frequency and for allocating content themes and visual media across a multitude of platforms in your monthly content calendar.

Frequency

Frequency is one of the top question topics we get from the audience when we speak at events—and for good reason. How often companies should post is not easy to generalize because it's going to be different for every company. Frequency will also be different for every channel your company has a presence on.

We're operating under the assumption that readers of this book already have a presence across multiple platforms and have done some work to determine their desired social media content frequency for each of them. You've made that determination probably based on things like how much relevant information you have to share and your resources, staffing, and ability to source visuals. Unless you're hardly posting at all, it makes sense to stick with that frequency as you ramp up your visual storytelling efforts. You've already built a benchmark based on how your content is currently performing, and consistency makes sense, especially in the beginning. Tinkering with your frequency is a good trial-and-error solution when you're looking to enhance engagement further into your program.

There have been a lot of different studies published over the past several years that show the best times to post on various networks. Just Google "best time to post," and you will see numerous different pieces of advice. Some say weekdays are the best days for engagement; others say weekends are. The data is controversial.

And while it's helpful to look at averages, frequency is unique for every company because of different fan counts, demographics, preferences, and levels of engagement. It's also a good idea to gauge the frequency of your competitors' posts as a way to understand if it's drastically different from your own—and if so, why? Also, your executives will inevitably ask, and you need to speak to how your approach differs and why. It's critical that you don't feel like you need to replicate the efforts of your competitors and that you instead remain focused on the best approach for your company.

If you are marketing in the United States, it's helpful to know that the Eastern and Central Time zones represent close to 80% of the U.S. population. If you have to make a choice which time zone to target, time things for your U.S. audiences in EST.

If you target international audiences, pay attention to which countries and time zones are most represented. When Ekaterina managed the Facebook strategy and global presence for Intel, she knew that her international audience was so diverse that no matter when she posted something, it would always get immediate likes and comments. But even then, she made sure she was using analytics to help her reach the highest peaks of engagement. First tracking it manually (in the early days), then engaging tools such as PageLever, she looked at the days and times when the most engagement happened.

It is also important to play with different times and to test what works best around various types of posts.

At the end of the day, quality content is always going to trump quantity and volume, especially with the ability across most social media platforms to use paid media to enhance the reach of a post or tweet. You never want to get caught in the cycle of producing content for content's sake, so frequency first and foremost needs to be in line with what's interesting, important, and relevant to your audience.

When evaluating frequency, a helpful metric to have is the shelf life, or life cycle, of your content by platform. Because each social media platform performs differently, measure your next 10 or so posts, tweets, Instagram photos, pins, and so on, on an hourly basis. Each hour, calculate how many engagements there are on the piece of content you posted—for example, likes, comments, shares, @replies, retweets, or repins. You may even need to go into shorter time increments for platforms like Twitter. Find out when that engagement starts to taper off and ultimately ends. Through this simple exercise, you'll better understand the shelf life of your content, which can help in determining the frequency per day and the time of day your content should be posted. You will also learn how to not step on your own toes by overposting so that you can give your content the optimal amount of time it needs to shine.

Usually the shelf life of a tweet is considered to be an hour at most, and shelf life of a Facebook post is about 24 hours.

Allocating Content Themes and Media

Once you have the frequency set, it's time to determine your monthly content mix. This is where you prioritize by social media platform the most important content themes that go into crafting your visual story. The mix needs to balance what's important from an ongoing visual storytelling perspective with goals, current events, questions, and general conversation from your customers. Rank these themes, and assign a frequency qualifier to each bucket, whether it's in terms of the number of posts or percentage of the month's content. This mix will likely be different by social media platform. It will also likely change each month depending on how much news your company has or the tweaks you're making in response to fan engagement.

When ranking these items, ensure that the mix has a balance to what you want your customers to know about you, versus what they're looking for. The content should also aim to be mostly upbeat, fun, motivating, and engaging. Remember that people don't always come online to read the newspaper. Sometimes they want to pet the cute dog too.

Once you have your monthly content themes outlined and prioritized, you can use this information as your baseline when you're crafting the actual visual content. Outlining content themes makes it easy to identify what messages will best be conveyed as photos, videos, infographics, presentations, and/or some other medium. Planning will also make your life overseeing social media easier: you won't be scrambling to get post content set or have to articulate your vision for content on the fly.

Planning for the Unexpected

We all understand how important yet challenging planning is given the realities of social media. Anything can happen at a moment's notice, like a crisis situation or a new meme taking the world by storm. Planning will help your company be more nimble to change as it hits. While this all sounds amazing, how do you actually plan for the unexpected?

The honest answer is that you're never going to predict everything that is going to happen. However, you can work with people in your company to identify common occurrences—both positive and negative—and look for opportunities to create visual content solutions around them. The proactive end of responding in real time to the latest viral sensation will be discussed in depth in Chapter 5. For the purposes of this chapter, we want to help you to identify how to anticipate key visual content opportunities in advance based on past history as you build up your content library.

In order to do this, you need to form a cross-department team of people who can help you to understand key themes or issues that have required a rapid response in the past. Typically this team will include people from brand and product marketing, public relations, and customer service.

Brand and Product Marketing

For brand and product marketing, you want to understand the most important factors that can influence sales and customer leads. For example, if you're a hardware shop, a heat wave may result in a sudden surge of sales for air-conditioning units and fans. Or a snowstorm will generate a rush to the store for shovels. When you're planning your content calendar ahead of time, this isn't necessarily stuff that you can write in, but it's important to your company. Identifying weather as an important theme around which to craft content to support key business goals allows you to get ahead of the game by crafting generic visual content around heat waves, snowstorms, dry spells, and other weather events. Save this content in your library for a rainy day—literally!

You should also ask the brand and product team about product perception, competitive positioning, and important trends or shifts in the industry coming up over the next year. All of these can result in a shift in strategy and present an opportunity to plan ahead with visual content.

Public Relations

For your public relations team, you want to have a strong sense of their annual plan and monthly focal points for pitching stories to the news media. These themes and points can not only generate additional ideas for your visual storytelling program but they can also help in maintaining a consistency of voice. The public relations team can also tip you off to the times of year for such events as key awards, rankings, events, executive speeches, exciting partnerships, and major announcements.

You should also ask your public relations team to think back over the past few years to the most common reactive issues facing your company. Everyone prefers to think about the fun and proactive side of social media, but the reality is that your business practices, values, employment policies, customer service issues, how and where you source your products, and other issues can all generate a negative wave of inquiries online from your customers. The purpose of this process is to better plan how you manage these sensitive situations online and if there is an opportunity to use visual content to help resolve them. Examples could include sourcing a how-to video in response to customer concerns about how a product or service works or to give customers a look inside the facility where your products are made. This practice will also help further strengthen your relationship with your PR team because all responses in relation to sensitive situations need to be consistent across traditional and online media.

Customer Service

Your customer service team is also an incredibly valuable resource when it comes to planning for the unexpected. Depending on how long your company has been around, they probably have on file years and years of customer inquiries and the company's responses to them. Understanding the most frequently asked customer service inquiries and comments—both positive and negative—can offer ideas for sourcing visual content. Based on past behavioral trends, it can also help your team to anticipate how visual content can better support frequently asked questions, a new product launch, store opening, and other similar events.

Ensuring that your content and daily social media community engagement is in line with customer service responses is also important for consistency as well. This team will be an important stakeholder should you ever need to manage through a social media crisis.

Ultimately, planning for the unexpected translates into planning for what you can anticipate. However, doing so will result in greater flexibility to jump on important trends that fall outside of your realm of predictability. Developing a robust content library and content buckets will free up the valuable time you need to allocate your creative resources around real-time opportunities when they arise.

Distribution and Engagement Strategy

Once you have your content calendar set and posts created, now comes the fun part: sharing it with your fans. When preparing to distribute your content, make sure someone from your company is there to listen and engage with feedback and responses. If you think of social media as an ongoing conversation, posting content without engagement can be likened to talking *at* versus *with* someone.

While the purpose of this book is to teach you the best practices of visual storytelling, half the fun of telling a story is watching the response from your audience in real time. From the cringes, to the laugh-out-loud moments or gasps of surprise, the best storytellers play off of their audience to really hit the message home and create a lasting experience.

You can and should be doing this as well on your social media channels. Use your visual storytelling program to spark one-to-one human conversations based on the content you're putting out. You've put a great deal of work into aligning your content with business goals and objectives, so your goal as a visual storyteller then becomes that of extending the life of the conversation and engagement for as long as it is relevant.

During these conversations, continue to wear your visual storytelling hat, and look for additional themes, ideas, or questions that will trigger more content ideas. It's also a good idea to actively look at the content your fans are sharing each day. Liking and commenting on visual content created by your fans—both positive and negative—can help to deepen your relationship with your consumers. It shows them that you're present and engaged yourself and that you care about the role your company, product, or service plays in their lives.

Crafting and Sourcing Stunning Visuals

In order to develop a cohesive visual marketing strategy, companies should be thinking like digital curators. When crafting visuals, the key is to personalize content across platforms, while keeping the tone and branding consistent. Regardless of budget or headcount, there are countless opportunities with visuals for driving creativity. In this section, we will share our top tips for developing different types of visuals, plus we'll give you some tools, apps, and other resources to help you along the way.

Traditional Images

In many ways, photography is like a blank canvas. Any moment can turn into a photo opportunity, with the beauty in the eye of the photographer. The concept of a well-composed photo is nothing new to companies— it's something they've been sourcing for their websites, advertisements, retail locations, and the news media for a long time. What's new, though, is the concept of social media–friendly images that drive an immediate response. For those looking to truly push the limits and take their imagery to the next level, check out our tips for taking stunning photos.

Like a Pro: 15 Tips for Social Media Photography

While you don't need a professional photographer on standby, you do need a steady hand and an understanding that practice makes perfect. Simply learn a few tips from the pros and companies that are generating best-in-class social imagery, and you'll be producing engaging images in no time.

1. **Up your resolution.** Make sure to start with the highest resolution possible, whether you're using a smartphone camera or a professional one. iPhones, for example, have a high dynamic range (HDR) setting, which results in a good quality image. When making collages, make sure the images are of a similar resolution. You can always diminish the resolution later as needed.

2. **Apply the rule of thirds.** Professional photographers recommend the *rule of thirds*, which means dividing up your image into thirds either horizontally or vertically and aligning your image slightly off center to make it more engaging.

3. **Variety matters.** They say variety is the spice of life, a mantra that rings true for your social media imagery. When snapping photos, always take more than you think you need, and take them in a range of angles, setups, and so on. If it helps, map out a storyboard or shot list of images you'll need to keep your team going during a photo shoot.

4. **Frame your shot.** Look for opportunities to create a natural frame around your images, whether it's with nature or with tangible items. If shooting from a wider angle, closely inspect everything that's happening in the background. In general, the less cluttered the background is, the better. This will make the image more exciting.

5. **Use closed-cropped images.** Close-cropped, uncluttered images allow the viewers to quickly and easily see what you're trying to showcase, whether it's mouthwatering food or the intricate details on a necklace.

6. **Work the angles.** Whether you're pointing up, down, straight on, to the left, or to the right, experiment with angling your images. A photo may become more

Like a Pro: 15 Tips for Social Media Photography, *continued*

engaging when shot at an angle versus straight on.

7. **Use a pop of color.** Whether it's a colorful backdrop or product, a pop of color helps an image to stand out.

8. **Shine bright with lighting and filters.** Make your images that much more dazzling by ensuring that your photos have good lighting and/or filters. With so many inexpensive and free options for editing your images, it has become easier to make your images stand out.

9. **Show—don't sell.** Not every image needs to feature products or to prompt the viewers to "buy now" or drive to the store. It's okay to celebrate a holiday occasion, share a great quote, or publish photos that relate back to your company's lifestyle.

10. **Inspire.** Through the use of images, inspire your community by showcasing your company's lifestyle, values, your leaders' opinions, or how your products and services are contributing to the greater good.

11. **Encourage emotion.** Whether it's cute puppies or an image of a father and son for Father's Day, don't be afraid to showcase your sentimental side when it's appropriate.

12. **Propel action.** With a hop, skip, or jump, infusing action into a still image can literally make it pop off the newsfeed.

13. **Sprinkle in humor.** Not every image has to be serious. Don't be afraid to have a little fun!

14. **Embrace creativity.** Not all images need to be of a singular item. Experiment with new ways to showcase your products or services. Mixing it up will make consumers pause and engage with the image.

15. **Go behind the scenes.** Give your fans a little something they don't usually see, whether it's your office, behind the scenes with a celebrity, or the amazing cupcakes your colleague made for someone's birthday. It will make your customers feel like a part of your brand.

Social Media Image Sizes by Platform

Wouldn't it be easy and efficient if all of your social media platforms accepted images of the same size? Unfortunately, we do not live in a one-size-fits-all social media world, so when it comes to curating social media imagery, size matters. Luckily for you, we've crafted a handy chart so you can keep all of the information at your fingertips.

Facebook

- **Cover photo.** 851 by 315 pixels. Start with a canvas of double that size—1,702 by 630—for sharp, crisp images. Facebook will resize it, and you'll have the right dimensions.

    Facebook recommends: to get the fastest load times for your page, upload an sRGB JPG file that's 851 pixels wide, 315 pixels tall, and less than 100 kilobytes. For images with your logo or for text-based content, you may get a higher-quality result by using a PNG file.

- **Profile picture.** Must be at least 180 by 180 pixels to upload. Facebook recommends: uploading a square image of your brand's logo. Rectangular images will be cropped to fit a square.
- **Profile thumbnail.** 90 by 90 pixels.
- **App tab images.** 111 by 74 pixels.
- **Timeline image.** 403 by 403 pixels.
- **Highlighted image.** 843 by 403 pixels.
- **Photo albums.** Photo albums can contain up to 1,000 photos. The maximum image size for uploading to your company albums or Timeline is **2,048 by 2,048 pixels**. The maximum display size within a photo album is **960 by 720 pixels** (landscape orientation).

Google+

- **Cover photo.** 2,120 by 1,192 pixels.
- **Profile photo.** 270 by 270 pixels.
- **Shared image.** 497 by 373 pixels.

Instagram
- **Profile photo.** 110 by 110 pixels.
- **Photo in feed.** 510 by 510 pixels.

LinkedIn
- **Cover photo.** 646 by 220 pixels.
- **Shared link image.** 180 by 110 pixels.
- **Products and services banner.** 646 by 220 pixels.
- **Careers cover photo.** 974 by 238 pixels.
- **Product image.** 100 by 80 pixels.

Pinterest
- **Profile photo.** 160 by 165 pixels.
- **Pins on main page.** 192 by scaled height.
- **Enlarged pin.** 600 by infinite pixels.
- **Board.** Large thumbnail 222 by 150 pixels.
- **Small board thumbnail.** 55 by 55 pixels.

Twitter
- **Profile picture.** 81 by 81 pixels.
- **Header image.** 520 by 260 pixels.
- **Background image.** Maximum file size of 2 megabytes.
  There really isn't a cap on the width or height of your Twitter background image, but if you make it too wide, most users won't be able to see whatever you put on the right-hand side.
- **Shared image.** 375 by 375 pixels.

YouTube
- **Channel icon.** 90 by 90 pixels.
  For best results, upload an 800 by 800 pixel image.
- **Cover art.** 2,560 by 1,440 pixels.

Tools to Help You Craft a Stunning Collage

Bazaart • A free app that pulls in your photos and Pinterest pins to create incredible, artistic collages. The collage can be saved to your camera roll and also shared across Pinterest, Facebook, Twitter, Instagram, Tumblr, and e-mail. Find it at http://www .bazaart.me.

Diptic • For $0.99 each, select from over 170 collage layouts, and then customize frames, filters, and text captions. There is also a range of editing options, plus sharing capabilities for use with e-mail or for posting directly to Instagram, Facebook, Flickr, Twitter, Tumblr, or any app that supports JPGs. Find it at http://www.dipticapp.com.

Fotor • A free tool for editing images, adding text, or creating collages. Images can be saved and shared across Facebook, Picasa, Tumblr, Flickr, and Twitter. Find it at http://www .fotor.com.

PicMonkey • A free tool for editing and adding filters, text, shapes, and more to images or for creating collages. Find it at http://www.pic monkey.com.

Photo Collages

Looking for inspiration on how to craft a collage? Look no further than the visual experience of your Instagram page. Ever since Instagram started offering a desktop viewing experience, it has showcased the value of the collage. Though arranged at random, you'll get a sense for just how engaging the right assortment of images can be when artfully placed together.

Collages have always been a natural fit for the fashion industry, inspired by the highly editorial nature of aligning images together to look like a magazine spread. Style inspiration community Polyvore practically runs on collages, both on its site and across its social media channels. Polyvore's collages offer a compelling example of how to artfully arrange your images and pops of colors to create a visual fashion story.

When making a collage, look closely at the balance of images, including their composition and colors. The idea is to pull the viewers in with a focal point but keep their interest with a range of colors, unique imagery, or visual focal points. It's also important that the imagery come together to craft a story, as several *Great Gatsby*–inspired collages from Polyvore show. One of the collages, for example, features a comfortable yet chic outfit for a lazy day that's a nod to 1920s fashion with the color themes of white, black, and yellow consistent throughout.

Many companies also leverage the creative power of collages to populate their Facebook or Google+ cover photos. With so much space to add images, a collage offers a nice way to maximize this real estate. It also doesn't have to be a full-on collage. It can be a series of images over a larger image.

Images with Text, Quotes, and Stats

When a photo alone won't do, text, quotes, and stats can help to clearly communicate a point, inspire your community, promote competitive differentiation, generate a laugh, and more.

1. **Clearly communicate a point.** Think about it. To its fans, a photo featuring a crushed can of Red Bull without text could mean a multitude of different things, from brute strength to anger, an unfortunate accident, and more. Layer in the text "We find your lack of energy disturbing," and the Instagram image takes on a new meaning in line with Red Bull's fun and extreme lifestyle.

2. **Inspire your community.** Whether it's a quote, stat, or phrase, the use of powerful words will deliver an inspiring message. Inspiring visual content can take many forms. Most often it's found in the form of a quote from a well-known thought leader, company executive, or customer. However, a powerful stat can bring a message or point of view to life. Depending on the intention of the post, a snappy one-liner like "Wish you were here" or "Love what you do" can also motivate your audience.

   Another idea is to produce a word cloud describing a value, product, or service. Want to go the extra mile? Consider crowdsourcing these words from your community.

3. **Promote competitive differentiation.** GE does a good job using visuals with quotes and statements to reinforce a key competitive differentiation—its people. Customer testimonials, positive press, research studies, awards, and third-party endorsements could also help to promote competitive differentiation.

4. **Generate a laugh.** While quotes inspire, stats reinforce key points and facts. Stats have the ability to add credibility, spark a

Tools for Adding Text to Images

Keep Calm-o-Matic • Love the Keep Calm and Carry On images? Create one for free with this easy-to-use website. Create a login to save final images. There's an ability to right click for a free image, but there is also a premium download option for $0.99 per image. Find it at http://www.keepcalm -o-matic.co.uk.

Over • Available for $1.99 for iPhone, iPod Touch, and iPad, this app allows users to easily add text to photos. It contains more than 200 fonts, and it can be shared across all social media platforms. Over also has a free version called Overgram with 30 fonts to select from. Find it at http://madewith over.com.

PicMonkey • This is a free tool for editing and adding filters, text, shapes, and more to images or for creating collages. Find it at http://www.picmonkey.com.

Pinstamatic • This free tool allows users to create and then pin website screen shots, customized quotes, custom sticky notes, songs from Spotify, Twitter profiles, calendar days, addresses, and images with personalized text or filters. **Tip:** right click on the image before pinning to Pinterest to save and share across additional social media channels. Find it at http://pinsta matic.com.

Quipio • This tool is available across iPhone, iPod Tough, and iPad for free. Described by TechCrunch as "Instagram for text messaging," this handy app is part social network, part useful tool. Easily combine photo and text, and share

Tools for Adding Text to Images, continued

the resulting image across Facebook, Instagram, Twitter, Weibo, SMS, e-mail, and the Quipo communities. Find it at https://quip.io.

QuotesCover.com • This free tool offers users the opportunity to source or create custom quotes that can be layered on images for Facebook or Google+ cover images or for Facebook or Twitter status updates. Quotes can be text only, or they can be layered onto an existing image. Find it at http://quotescover.com.

WordFoto • This app for iPhone and iPad Touch turns photos and words into amazing typographic works of art. The app is $1.99, and users can upload images from an album or their camera roll. Users have the option of saving, e-mailing, or sharing on Facebook. The end results are a mosaiclike image that's highly creative and attention-grabbing. Find it at http://www.wordfoto.com.

WordCamPro • This app allows Android users to turn their images into amazing typographic art using text. Users can select between using one or several fonts to communicate single letters, single words, or multiple-word phrases. The photo is created from scratch using any phrase the user would like. The result can be saved, and it can be shared across social media sites. WordCam Pro ranges between $0.99 and $1.99. Find it on Google Play.

TIPS *for Adding Text, Quotes, and Stats to Social Media Images*

1. **Use text as needed.** If your image communicates your desired story without text, then it probably isn't needed. But if words or numbers will help viewers to fully understand the context or if they will add a humorous punch line that isn't conveyed through the image, then go for it.

2. **Determine your desired outcome.** Whether inspiring, comforting, entertaining, or making them laugh, what do you want your audience to do after seeing your visual with a text, quote, or stat together?

3. **Strike a balance.** Keep the message brief and powerful. Make sure there's a good ratio of image to text, quote, or stat—strive for achieving perfect harmony versus competing for attention.

4. **Crowdsource inspiration.** Is there a frequently used word, question, quote, hashtag, or phrase to describe your products or services? Consider looking to your online community for inspiration on ways to mix in one-liners, quotes, polls, or stats to complement your visuals.

5. **Ask questions.** Looking for a quick focus group? For text posts, embed a question on an image, and let the consumer feedback help influence a product or business decision.

6. **Do your homework.** Found a quote you love? A great stat to use? Just make sure to fully vet the person behind the quote and make sure he or she is a good fit to represent your brand on a visual piece of content. It's also critical to understand how the stats were sourced to ensure their credibility.

7. **Get crunching.** Does your company save consumers a certain amount of money or time on average? Could the amount of sandwiches you sell per year circle the globe? Get your in-house mathematical whiz to help you crunch numbers and come up with stats and fun facts that will make a difference with your customer base.

conversation, or call attention to an important topic or issue. As seen with one of Coca-Cola's posts, stats can also be downright silly. Citing "An ice cube's confidence increases up to 500% when it's served in a Coke," this lighthearted stat shared on the company's Instagram account and complementary image prove that it's okay to have a little fun with your social media community.

Postcards and E-cards

With people increasingly reliant on electronic devices, the traditional postcard has had to transform for the digital age. While the medium may have changed, postcards and e-cards still offer a strong opportunity to craft a visual story built around an occasion or experience.

Hyatt House, part of the Hyatt Hotel chain, treated guests during their stay with two complimentary postcards from Postagram. Housed on an app on both Postagram's and Hyatt House's Facebook pages, guests could add a personalized photo, a 180-character message, a name, and an address. The postcard was then printed and mailed to the recipient. The campaign was created as a way to help Hyatt House build deeper relationships with its guests by showcasing that it understood the importance of keeping friends and family top of mind while on the road.

It's hard not to align a postcard or e-card with a holiday occasion. Holidays like Christmas, Valentine's Day, Mother's Day, and Father's Day all have us feeling more sentimental and thus more interested in reaching out to the people we care about the most. But what if you accidently,

Tools for Creating and Sending Postcards

Cards in the Post • With Cards in the Post, sending high-quality personalized pictures by mail is really quick and really easy. You can grab pictures from Instagram, Facebook, Google, or Flickr. You can use this site on a desktop, laptop, tablet, or mobile phone. There's no installing apps or anything like that. No account to set up. Just speedy to use, easy, and fun too. Find it at http://www.cardsinthepost.com.

SnapShot Postcard • Share the memories stored in your photos by sending custom picture postcards. With SnapShot Postcard, you build your own postcard right on your iPhone, iPad, iPod, or Android device. Find it at http://www.snapshotpostcard.com.

TIPS *for Social Media Postcards*

- **Outline communications goals.** A postcard or e-card is essentially a communication to your consumers. What do you want them to take away from the communication? A thank-you, key product message, or inspiring words? Or do you want to make them laugh?

- **To share or not to share.** Having your postcard or e-card shared should be a key goal when using this medium. Make sure your user experience is designed to be easily shareable and that it has a clear call to action.

- **Invest in quality visuals.** Make sure the images used are eye-catching and in line with the photo best practices shared earlier in the chapter. The better the quality, design, and overall layout of a postcard or e-card, the stronger the experience will be for your end user.

- **Keep the message simple.** Too much text will overwhelm a postcard or e-card. Short, sweet, and to the point resonate the best. Let the visuals shine, and have the text be complementary.

- **Embrace seasonality.** Whether it's a specific time of year or it's a reminder note from a service provider, postcards and e-cards can capture the spirit of the season and motivate sharing in a way that other media cannot.

- **Pleasant reminder.** If you're a service provider trying to send an appointment reminder, or you're a business trying to promote a sale or limited time offering, an e-card or postcard can offer a quick, easy, and highly visual way to get the message across.

- **Mix digital and physical.** Similar to Hyatt House's example, being able to create a two-sided tangible piece of content to surprise and delight someone in the mail can offer a lot of value to your customers. Especially if you can put a call to action on the card to tweet a thank-you message to the sender. If mixing the two, make sure to brand and offer unique visual experiences on both sides of the postcard.

- **Reward customers.** Postcards and e-cards can also be used as a way to thank your most loyal customers. From sending a simple thank-you note or an exclusive coupon or offer, people love feeling special, and this medium offers an easy way to send this type of communication.

or not so accidently, offended someone over the course of the year and want to make amends?

Simply make a Peeps Offering.

Created by the iconic Peeps candy, the company wanted to remind fans that it was also around during the December holiday season. In order to break through the holiday clutter, Peeps offered its fans on Facebook a chance to send tongue-in-cheek e-cards with one-liners like these: "I'm sorry I defriended you. Again." Or "I'm sorry for using mistletoe as an excuse to kiss your Mom." Laugh-out-loud funny, the Peeps Offering campaign showcases how e-cards can help to show the lighter side of your company.

Memes

Although memes are definitely one of the easiest forms of content marketing, *memenic marketing* isn't as simple as it first appears. As with any other campaign, it helps to be strategic when choosing and putting out a message about your brand. It's also important that the end result be fun and irreverent.

Most memes make light of situations and human behavior. When brainstorming meme ideas, it's ok to "memejack" and create your own play on the popular themes of the moment. The key is to do it in a clever and original way. People love seeing how others take wacky meme ideas to the next level, so this may seem obvious, but use your own photo, and don't copy existing memes word for word. Try to bring your own voice and brand personality through both the copy and the visual.

Commonly Used Memes
- **Cats or dogs.** Make a cat or dog versus a person the hero—anything goes! Grumpy Cat and Lolcats are especially popular memes.
- **Challenge accepted.** For example, "You can't stay in bed all day. / Challenge accepted."

Tools for Creating Memes

Memes are not hard to create if you have an image and tools to overlay text onto an image (see the tools in the "Images with Text, Quotes, and Stats" part of this chapter). Most memes use the Impact font in white with a 3- to 5-point black outline, which is very easy to overlay on an image. If you're looking for additional resources, here are three websites to consider:

MemeGenerator.net. • Select from preexisting character images, or upload your own. This is a free tool, so you'll need to create a custom name for your character that will live on the site for others to use, and then you can add text to the meme and share it across Facebook, Twitter, Reddit, Pinterest, and Tumblr. Just note that a "MemeGenerator .net" light gray watermark appears on the bottom right corner. Find it at http://meme generator.net.

QuickMeme.com and weknowmemes .com • Both sites allows you to select from already generated images and add personalized text to them. This is a free tool, and it is helpful if you want to play off of already successful meme images. However, doing so may not be feasible depending on how strict your legal department is. Find it at http:// www.quickmeme.com and http://weknow memes.com/generator.

- **Common situations.** For example, funny responses to asking someone out, waking up, office humor, things kids do, celebrating holiday occasions, and more.
- **Confessions.** For example, "I do / Use your toothbrush."
- **First-world problems.** For example, "I lost my phone. / Now I have to use my BlackBerry."
- **Flashbacks.** For example, 1970s, 1980s, 1990s moments.
- **Good or bad luck.** For example, "Put on old jeans. / Found $$$ in the pocket."
- **Like a boss.** Can be used when conquering an everyday situation in a big way.
- **Personalities.** For example, the jerk, the crazy girlfriend, the terrible boss, and the hysterical statements they make.
- **Song one-liners.** For example, Jepsen's "Call Me Maybe" or Gotye's "Somebody I Used to Know."
- **TV shows and movies.** For example, funny one-liners from popular TV shows and movies. Reality TV is a well-known source for amazing meme one-liners.
- **What if I told you.** Funny, sarcastic, and very frank statements on common occurrences.

TIPS *to Help Companies Embrace Memes*

1. **Understand memes.** Understand what they are, how they work, and which memes appeal to which audiences. Think about whether your audience regularly shares content online, and research the pain points, misconceptions, and common issues they experience.

2. **Pay attention to the memes that are popular right now.** Look for memes that are just beginning to get popular (hint: memes from movies or TV shows that have a lot of hype or have just been released). Memes are already viral; so half your work has already been done. It's just up to you to come up with something funny and relevant that works within the framework of the meme.

3. **Use humor.** Memes are predominantly an entertainment vehicle, so you'd better be making your audience laugh. Test your memes before releasing them to check that they're funny enough to work for your audience.

4. **Ensure that the tone and message of the meme jibe with your brand.** But don't be *so* branded that your message can't be shared. Memes should express sentiments that adhere to real pain points

expressed by your buyers but without pushing a solution. Many businesses have gotten into trouble by publishing memes that don't gel with the core values of their audience (for example, sarcasm and black humor directed at a wholesome audience, or political or racial jokes that alienate audience members).

5. **Make it visible.** You can share your meme on your social media pages—Facebook, Pinterest, Twitter, Tumblr, or Google+. You can also add it to meme sharing sites and encourage your followers to share on social bookmarking sites like Reddit. Use hashtags associated with your meme to make your meme easy to find. This is particularly important on Tumblr because tags are the predominant means of searching on that site. If you are creating a whole series of memes around a central character, you could even create a blog or social media page for that character, as Home Depot did for Richard the Cat.

6. **Use memes to create value-added content.** If you're not sure what to share on your Facebook page, creating and sharing memes related to your customer base or products can be great ways to generate

(continued)

TIPS *to Help Companies Embrace Memes,* *continued*

interest in your brand. Creating memes is usually a lot simpler than blogging or creating video or infographics.

7. **Run a meme creation contest.** Have your audience generate memes based on a particular image or video. Sharing all the entries on your social media pages and meme-generation sites will give you weeks or months of user-generated content, and it will help you reach a wider audience because the contestants will share their entries with their networks.

- **What people think I do/What I really do.** Funny way to mock a difference in perception between what people think you do versus what you actually do.

One idea is to embrace a fun personality related to your company or brand. It could be a spokesperson, mascot, even a personable office pet. For example, Dos Equis's famous "Most Interesting Man in the World"

ads have his own hysterical and sometimes racy series of memes. Remarkably, these memes are not generated by Dos Equis. Its community of enthusiastic fans generates the memes. Though amazing, wouldn't it be nice to start or add to the trend? Create your own by introducing the cute office puppy who chews shoes and won't let anyone near his favorite stuffed animal as the newest shareable meme sensation.

"What People Think I Do/What I Really Do" is another great example of a meme that can be used effectively by brands to address misconceptions about a product or service. HubSpot used this meme to great success on its Facebook page, generating hundreds of likes and shares.

GIFs

GIFs can help bring a static image to life by fusing images together to create animation-like motion. Companies can use GIFs to create bite-sized stories around products, events, and funny one-liners and actions, whether it's a model strutting down a runway, a cake being decorated, or a motivational quote. Common themes like having a "case of the Mondays," "TGIF," or seasonal holidays can spark creative GIFs. Companies can also embrace the animation quality of GIFs by parsing together historical content to show then versus now or to give a quick example of how a product or service works.

Common Themes for GIFs
- **Celebrity moments.** From Beyoncé to the Kardashians, President Obama, and more, a quick movement, pose, or dance move from a celebrity can instantly spread like wildfire in a GIF.
- **Cute animals.** Whether cuddling, chasing their tails, or bouncing off the walls, cute animals are GIF gold.
- **Food.** Who doesn't love bringing their foodie cravings to life? Think of a slow-motion GIF featuring an ooey gooey slice of cheese pizza being pulled away from the pie, or chocolate sauce being drizzled over an ice cream sundae.
- **Nostalgia.** Remember the TV shows, toys, and pop stars that you grew up with? People love traveling back in a virtual time machine through GIFs to tap into nostalgia from way back when.
- **My reaction to.** Similar to a meme, users take popular and wacky pop culture reactions GIFs and use them to communicate how they feel about events in their lives. If they're upset, they may show a celebrity

Tools for Creating GIFs

Photoshop • This program still reigns supreme as a tool to create GIFs.

Giffing Tool • This GIF-maker was developed for speed and ease. Simply drag across your screen to record movies, YouTube videos, and even existing GIFs. Find it at http://www.giffingtool.com.

GIFboom • This application allows you to create animated photos (GIFs) from your camera or your photo library or your videos in 60 seconds! You can send the GIFs to your friends via e-mail, multimedia messaging service (MMS), or social media network. Find it at http://gifboom.com.

Cinemagram • This application that allows you to create fun, short videos. You can share them instantly to Tumblr, Twitter, and Facebook. Find it at http://cinemagr.am.

GIF Brewery • This application lets you convert brief clips from your video files into GIFs. Find it at http://www.helloresolven.com/portfolio/gifbrewery/.

GIF SHOP • This allows you to make animated GIFs for your iPhone! Find it at http://gifshop.tv.

Gifninja • This web-based tool lets you upload either a video clip or a series of still images to construct your animation. Find it at http://gifninja.com.

Picasion • This web-based tool lets you upload a maximum of 10 images, or alternatively, import up to 50 images directly from Flickr or Picasa. Find it at http://picasion.com.

throwing a hissy fit, or if they're happy, they might show a GIF of an athlete doing a victory dance.

- **Pop culture phenomena.** From McKayla Maroney's "not impressed" to President Obama's fist bump, GIFs bring to life action-oriented pop culture phenomena.
- **Statements.** Similar to memes, people use GIFs to highlight something visually about their personality, usually taken from pop culture such as, "My mom thinks I'm awesome," "I'm kind of a big deal," or "Haters gonna hate."

- **Stunts and sports.** The action capabilities of a GIF make it easy to share the game-winning shot or an unbelievable stunt in a short-form animation.
- **TV shows, movies, and music videos.** GIF enthusiasts often parse pivotal scenes in TV shows, movies, and music videos. Add in text, and you can relive a favorite moment over and over.

Infographics

While the case for using infographics as part of a visual storytelling program is strong, it's a medium that cannot be forced. All of the factors—data, design, visuals, layout, and color—must come together harmoniously.

Though they are free and rather easy to use, we recommend working with a designer to build your own, custom-branded infographic. Since this is a popular medium, it is critical to ensure the visual represents your brand well.

Tools for Creating Infographics

Infogr.am • This popular platform has seen thousands of infographics created to date. Infogr.am is nice and simple, and it has a lot of power-packed features. Find it at http://infogr.am.

InfoActive • This platform helps users build interactive infographics and live data visualizations. Find it at https://infoactive.co.

Easel.ly • This tool takes a theme-based, drag-and-drop approach to infographic creation, with a small selection of just "vhemes" (visual themes). Find it at http://www.easel.ly.

Piktochart • Create an innovative infographic using a combination of different types of visualizations: themes, icons, images, and charts exporter. Find it at http://piktochart.com.

Visual.ly • This is an easy-to-use tool for creating custom infographics. Find it at http://create.visual.ly.

iCharts • Use this to create great looking charts in minutes with interactive and easy-to-share data. Find it at http://www.icharts.net.

TIPS *for Designing Infographics*

1. **Data matters.** Data and research quality are of the utmost importance and should be carefully selected when considering an infographic. It's important that all data or research displayed in an infographic be clearly disclosed and cited. Without solid data or research to back up your points, you shouldn't go down the path of making an infographic.

2. **Developing a storyboard.** When starting the process of creating an infographic, it's recommended that a storyboard be created to determine the layout and information flow. Parse the key data points and how they can be shaped into a larger, impactful message. If the story you're trying to tell doesn't resonate at this stage, it's not going to make a good infographic. Good stories have a beginning, middle, and an end, all of which should be communicated in an infographic.

3. **Format and layout.** Once you have your storyboard set, consider the best way to format it. Sites Visual.ly and Infogr.am offer free tools to help you think through how to design an infographic. While most infographics are vertical, they can also be designed horizontally or in both formats to increase the infographic's shareworthiness across social media platforms. Pinterest, for example, favors vertical infographics, but a horizontal infographic can work better on Facebook through the highlighting or cover photo features.

4. **Design elements.** For content, factors like typography, colors, and visuals bring the data to life. The right typography, or text, can make or break the visual experience. It's also important to have a snappy title that attracts attention. Color selection is also incredibly important. It's recommended to avoid a white background and to avoid dominant dark colors and neons when possible. When in doubt, less is more in the color department, and using three well-selected colors works very well. If you need to use more, adding different shades of those three colors will complement the look and feel.

   It's also important to pay attention to the design elements incorporated in the information flow. In order to most resonate with the viewers, make the key hook or takeaway of your infographic pop, and place it at the center

TIPS *for Designing Infographics,* continued

or very end. Carefully look through each visual element in your infographic. If it doesn't add value to the overall story, it's not worth including.

5. **Test it.** It's also important to set up your infographic for success by testing its viewing experience on multiple screens and social media platforms, including desktops, tablets, and other mobile devices. To ensure that your content is easy to understand, consider enlisting a group of colleagues or friends to make sure your message comes across clearly.

User-Generated Content

With the rise in visual social media platforms, many companies are now turning to their consumers to source user-generated images and videos. As previously seen in this book, companies like Lululemon, Coach, Coca-Cola, Burberry, Nike, and more are all successfully using user-generated content (UGC) to participate in collaborative visual storytelling with their customers. Look closely at the examples shared, and you'll see that the key to encouraging user-generated content is knowing your customer base. You need to understand what imagery or videos you can encourage, plus the level of depth or creativity. In order to achieve your desired results, it's also vital to create a forum with a clear call to action and to communicate how fans can participate and submit images.

TIPS *to Get Your Company Sourcing and Sharing User-Generated Content*

1. **Question sharing habits.** Determine what types of visual content your fans are sharing about your company and what the volume looks like. You need to pass the "give a darn" factor with your fans in order to collect the best-quality user-generated content. If it's not natural for your fans to share visual content about your company, you'll face a higher barrier to entry. Alternatively, user-generated images or videos can work against a company if its products do not meet consumer expectations, so pay close attention to sentiment before jumping into a UGC campaign.

2. **Reward behavior.** If you need an extra boost to encourage consumers to share user-generated content, you may want to launch your campaign with a contest to try and seed the behavior with your core audience. Following the contest, share as many compelling images, videos, and so on as possible to further encourage the behavior from your community. Going forward, sprinkle in further contests, or surprise-and-delight rewards as a way to thank your loyal fans for participating.

3. **Look for themes.** If you're a company that already sees a lot of compelling images or videos from your social community, then pay close attention to the most common types of photo and videos and hashtags used. What visual story is being told about your company? Is it in line with the visual story you want to be told? How does the image or video sentiment skew—positive, negative, or neutral? Use these key learnings to shape your strategy around this user behavior to form a more fan-centric campaign.

4. **Identify the pros, cons, and potential for hijacks.** When considering a user-generated content campaign, carefully evaluate the pros, cons, and potential for hijacks. The pros need to align with key business objections and spell out how the user-generated content will add value to your visual storytelling goals. The cons would relate to things like barriers to entry, negative sentiments, costs to your company, and the potential to take your campaign in a direction that you don't want it to go in. Though not overly common, UGC hijacks can happen. As a result,

TIPS *to Get Your Company Sourcing and Sharing User-Generated Content,* *continued*

it's important to look closely at the call to action and form an internal focus group to determine any potential for misunderstanding or overriding a promotion.

5. **Choose a clear call to action.** In order to reduce the barrier to entry, choose your call to action and designated hashtag wisely. Consumers need to know that they're opting into your UGC promotion, so it's recommended that the hashtag be unique and campaign specific. Though obvious, make sure you check your desired hashtag ahead of time across all social media channels—you would be surprised how many companies do not! Make sure to avoid a hashtag that already has a lot of uses.

6. **Make full disclosure.** One of the reasons consumers participate in user-generated campaigns is for social validation, but don't take their interest in starring on your social media channels for granted. Make sure consumers understand how and where the photos or videos will be used to prevent any upsets or potential backlash. If you're collecting images or videos from Facebook, Twitter, and Instagram but you also want to share them on your website, Tumblr, and Pinterest, make sure your participants are aware of that. As evidenced by the hysteria when consumers believed that Instagram was claiming ownership of their personal photos on the platform, it's clear that the knowledge of the use and terms of submission are vital to a successful campaign.

7. **Seed examples.** Looking for specific types of images or videos from a user-generated campaign? Seed examples of the types of imagery or videos you're looking for to help ensure quality and motivate your desired results. Throughout the campaign, make sure to pulse in submitted images or videos from your community to further generate excitement and awareness. When highlighting examples, it's important to show a range in order to inspire creativity.

8. **Give rewards and recognition.** While not all UGC campaigns are run as contests, it certainly doesn't hurt to celebrate your fans with rewards and recognition. It could be a featured image of the week,

(continued)

TIPS *to Get Your Company Sourcing and Sharing User-Generated Content,* *continued*

or it could be randomly sending fans that participate something special as a thank-you. This will help to further deepen your relationships with your consumers. Just make sure that any note and package is put together with a careful attention to detail because most consumers will snap and share an image of it on their social media channels. This offers a great opportunity to generate additional world-of-mouth buzz from your fans.

9. **Moderate the workflow plan.** Though user-generated content is often credited for being low cost, it's worth noting that using tools or third-party moderation and approval support does require an investment. Alternatively, managing a user-generated content initiative in-house will also require a time commitment, depending on the volume of entries received, process for securing approvals, and other factors. Make sure you plan for the time or monetary commitment required before going down a UGC path.

Tools for Collecting User-Generated Content

FeedMagnet • FeedMagnet is a content marketing and curation platform leveraging the best of social, user-generated, and real-time content across all of the major social media platforms including Facebook, Twitter, Google+, Instagram, Vine, Pinterest, LinkedIn, YouTube, Tumblr, Foursquare, Vimeo, and Salesforce Chatter. Notable clients include Ben & Jerry's, Farmers Insurance, Sephora, VMWare, and General Electric. Find it at http://www.feedmagnet.com.

Mass Relevance • Mass Relevance is a social experience platform for brands and media to drive real-time, relevant, and curated social content experiences to engage audiences on any digital surface. Mass Relevance has the ability to pull data from multiple sources including Twitter, Facebook, Instagram, Google+, and YouTube. Notable clients include Xbox, Pepsi, TicTac, KPMG, Patagonia, and Foot Locker. Find it at http://www.massrelevance.com.

Olapic • Olapic's mission is to help put user-generated photos where they belong—on your website! Olapic enables any site to collect, curate, and display user-generated photos. Olapic sources images from the most popular photo sharing networks, including Facebook, Instagram, Twitter, and Flickr. Notable clients include Lululemon, New Balance, People Magazine, Sony, and Threadless. Find it at http://www.olapic.com.

Seen • Seen is a platform that connects businesses with consumers through visual media, including hashtag-driven Instagram and Twitter photo campaigns. Seen gives brands valuable insights into their social communities and brand-relevant conversations through user-generated photo sharing, which enables them to connect with fans in new and more meaningful ways. Notable clients include Indianapolis Motor Speedway, ESPN, Dodge Ram, Ford, and Bath & Body Works. Find it at http://seenmoment.com.

Videos: YouTube, Instagram, and Vine

From YouTube to Instagram, Vine, and others, companies have choices as never before for capturing and sharing videos. Furthermore, all of the major social media platforms from Facebook to Twitter, Google+, Pinterest, Tumblr, and even SlideShare also make it easy to stream video—with the engagement rates to match. This offers a unique value proposition and business case for companies to use video to tell their stories. The challenge and opportunity for companies is to define the role video will play as part of their visual storytelling program.

Our recommendation is that you revert back to your content calendar planning and look at the top opportunities for which video is going to help tell your visual story in a way that other media cannot. You don't want to get caught up in all the things you could be doing. Instead, focus on what is the most strategic. Think about your target audience, desired end goals, and resources available. How can video bring to life important supporting themes in your visual storytelling program and make the greatest impact?

Look closely at the common types of video and see what your company would prioritize as part of your visual storytelling program.

Common Types of Videos
- Announcements
- Behind-the-scenes scoops
- Case studies
- Celebrity partnerships
- Community involvement
- Company overview
- Demos
- Event highlights
- FAQs
- Goals
- How-tos
- Live streams

TIPS *for Incorporating Video into a Visual Storytelling Program*

1. **Evaluate audience needs.** Videos offer a more personal, conversational way to reach your audience. In order to captivate their attention, you need to adopt an audience-first mentality. This is precisely the reason why glossy, overproduced corporate videos do not resonate, but videos featuring the Old Spice Guy or Evian's dancing babies do. They're real, they're funny, and they communicate in an entertaining way.

   This is not to say that every video needs to be funny or wacky. The Boston-area B2B company Grasshopper produced an amazing video titled *Entrepreneurs Can Change the World* in support of a phone system targeted at entrepreneurs. Moving, yet simple and easy to follow, the video secured over 1 million views for its inspirational tone. It also helped the Grasshopper break through the clutter and make a name for itself, all because the company crafted its video in a way that would resonate with the target audience.[5]

2. **Show off your personality.** Think for a moment about your favorite conference speakers or online videos. Sure, production quality, story flow, and so on matter, but personality seals the deal. Even if you're a very serious company, review the list "XYZ Company Voice and Personality" earlier in this chapter, and make sure your desired traits and values shine through in your videos. And, as companies like Blendtec have showcased, it's okay to have a fun-loving side. Just make sure it's authentic and it doesn't come off like you're trying too hard!

3. **Mix it up.** YouTube, Instagram, and Vine—all three platforms cater to different types and lengths of videos. For example, you might host a how-to video on YouTube, but you would share a behind-the-scenes clip of the making of the video on Instagram and capture an abbreviated version in 6 seconds on Vine.

   Spend some time reading through our Chapter 3 on the best practices, features, and case studies on how companies activate on YouTube, Instagram, and Vine as you evaluate the videos you want to produce. Each has different strengths and weaknesses, plus they all integrate

(continued)

TIPS *for Incorporating Video into a Visual Storytelling Program,* *continued*

differently with social media platforms like Facebook and Twitter. Each social media platform appeals to different audiences, so think strategically about the types of videos produced, as well as their lengths and the platforms used. Doing so can help you reach different audiences while showing different aspects of your personality.

4. **Have a distribution strategy.** So you made a great video for YouTube. Now what? As mentioned in this chapter, the proliferation of social media platforms means that just because your video lives on one site or platform, that doesn't mean it can't be shared across others. Your distribution strategy for your video needs to be factored in during the planning process. Videos from sites like Instagram and Vine are also saved to your camera roll, so make sure that those settings are enabled in each app. Even if it's only a 6- or 15-second video, it could still potentially be edited into a longer video, or it could be tweaked to include music and so on to extend its shelf life.

5. **Source user-generated video content.** The UGC phenomenon is not limited to photos alone. More than ever, companies are turning to their customers and fans to share user-generated videos. Platforms like Vine now allow companies to revine (like retweet) videos posted by their fans. There are a number of companies that we listed earlier in this chapter in the "User-Generated Content" section that help to collect user-generated video content. Companies like Tongal have also emerged to help run user-generated video contests. There's certainly a higher barrier to entry with UGC video contests, but if you're looking for quality versus quantity, it is a good path to pursue.

- Office tours
- Parodies
- Testimonials
- Video blogs
- Visual portfolios

Measurement

As discussed throughout this chapter, measurement will play an ongoing role in the life cycle of your visual storytelling program. Any time you embark on a new initiative with visual content, trial and error and testing are going to play a starring role. This is not a bad thing! In fact, the ability to take calculated risks and embrace creative new ways to structure your visual storytelling efforts is going to be key to long-term success.

Truth be told, we could fill another book with tips and techniques on how to measure your visual storytelling efforts. In the interest of brevity, if you continue to track, measure, analyze, and tweak your visual content on the fly based your community's responses, you will be able to paint a picture internally of how this initiative is improving your social media efforts.

Take every win and setback as a learning opportunity, and showcase how those learnings have resulted in the continued evolution of your visual storytelling strategy. Even for the most celebrated companies, success and staying relevant are ongoing processes. It's easy to get comfortable and stuck in a specific approach, so think of measurement as a check and balance for keeping yourself honest.

Use the tools and recommendations provided earlier in this chapter as a start, but consider personalizing them to what your senior leadership is asking about. To dig deeper on social media measurement, we recommend the following books written by experts in the field of social media analytics:

- Leslie Poston, *Social Media Metrics for Dummies*
- Chuck Hemann and Ken Burbary, *Digital Marketing Analytics: Making Sense of Consumer Data in a Digital World*
- Olivier Blanchard, *Social Media ROI: Managing and Measuring Social Media Efforts in Your Organization*

CHAPTER 5

Real-Time Marketing in a Visual World

Your brand is turning 100 years old, and you want to celebrate. You also want to show that your brand is just as relevant to its customers as it has always been, but how do you make the centenary commemoration strike a chord with a younger, more tech-aware audience? The classic cookie producer Oreo managed to achieve all of this—and to win new fans in the process.

In 2012, over 100 days—one for each year of the brand's history—Oreo's creative team crafted an image that reflected one of the day's trending news stories. Called the Daily Twist, the story would be given a playful and fun Oreo theme and shared across the brand's social media channels with the hashtag #DailyTwist.

This example of a brand's agility, on-the-fly thinking, and in a lot of cases, fast response showcases what has recently been referred to as *real-time marketing* (RTM), *agile marketing, on-the-fly marketing,* or *real-time social response.* Oreo listened to what was important to its audience, and

> There is a gold mine of social data available to marketing departments, but it takes the right tools, analytics, and mostly, the right mentality to make use of it in real time. Brands that are changing their marketing strategies to integrate real-time social listening and social data are beginning to see amazing results. But real-time marketing goes deeper than humorous visual responses or witty videos. It's about responsiveness, truly knowing your customers, and taking a flexible approach to marketing.

> Real-time marketing isn't just for the trendy, consumer-facing brands. It is a way of thinking that goes to the heart of your brand's ethos and creates a meaningful and human conversation between companies and consumers.

within hours the creative team put together a visual that showed Oreo's take on it. Of course, some events could have been anticipated in advance, such as a holiday or a film release, but others such as a Loch Ness Monster photo hitting the news or five gold medals won in a day at the Olympics were created in response to the current events that were important to Oreo's audience.

Oreo created images that celebrated everything from national holidays to real-time events with image titles reading "Talk like a pirate day," "National radio day," "Elvis week," "Mars Rover lands," "Horse dance goes viral," "Pride," "Anniversary of first high five," "National Bullying Prevention month," "The Dark Knight rises in theaters tomorrow," "Comic-Con begins," and so on. You can find the full collection of images here: http://www.pinterest.com/oreo/daily-twist.

How did social media respond to the Daily Twist images?

Over the campaign there were 433 million Facebook views with an increase in shares of 280%, creating 231 million media impressions and making Oreo the brand with the highest buzz increase in 2012 (+49%).

The campaign also won one of the two Cyber Grand Prix awards at the Cannes International Festival of Creativity.[1]

Picture behind the scenes at a brand such as Oreo that has integrated real-time marketing into its strategy: marketing departments flexible enough to respond to events as they happen and tailor their marketing accordingly; to monitor customer opinion and tweak campaigns in the light of it; to make product decisions based on data collected minute by minute; to be able to put together an accurate picture of how products and campaigns are received—not just with sales figures but with accurate social media data from actual or potential customers.

There is a gold mine of social data available to marketing departments, but it takes the right tools, analytics, and mostly, the right mentality to make use of it. Brands that are changing their marketing strategies to integrate real-time social listening and social data are beginning to see the results—but it's still in the early days, and many companies aren't yet convinced that its of relevance to them. The sorts of examples that are frequently held up—clever images that reference a current event that go viral on Twitter—might not seem significant to many organizations. But RTM goes deeper than humorous visual responses or witty videos. It's about responsiveness, truly knowing your customers, and taking a flexible approach to marketing.

Think what that could mean to a brand:

> Embracing real-time marketing completes, for your business, the true potential of social marketing.
> **—PAUL O'BRIEN,** Dachis Group[2]

- Serving customers relevant advertising messages that they may truly be interested in
- Personalized customer service
- Research, development, or alteration of products based on an in-depth knowledge of customer needs
- Instant access to a wealth of real-time market research
- Marketing campaigns that reflect the public mood or even set new trends
- Connecting with potential customers based on their social profiles and conversations

We are at the beginning of a new era in marketing, one that has its finger on the pulse of consumers and can make decisions and implement them rapidly. We have an ability to know our customers as never before: what they want, what they are saying, and how they are thinking.

Why are we devoting a whole chapter of this book on the topic of visual marketing to RTM specifically? Because so many RTM strategies and tactics—and certainly almost

STATS

69% of B2B marketers rated "creating original content" as their biggest content marketing challenge.[3]

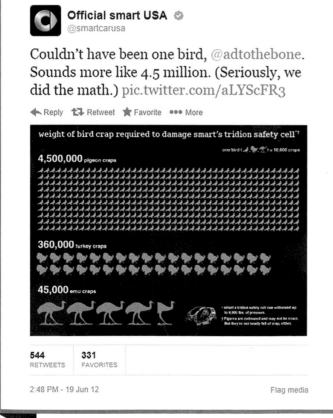

© Courtesy of Daimler AG.

all of the best ones—involve rich media. As you can see from the Oreos example above, to be truly effective, brands are using images, videos, and infographics as a real-time social response, based on the current interests and needs of their audiences.

What Is Real-Time Marketing?

Constant, relevant content creation can be hard work for brands.

But Smart Car shows just how real-time marketing techniques can inspire ideas for creative content—and turn product criticism into an opportunity to drive engagement *and* share important product data at the same time.

In June 2012 Clayton Hove, creative director for an ad agency in North Dakota, sent the tweet you see above, left.

What was Smart Car's inspired response?

"Couldn't have been one bird, @adtothebone. Sounds more like 4.5 million. Seriously, we did the math." And they attached the infographic showing exactly that math.

The clever graph, which showed exactly how much bird crap it would take to damage a Smart Car's safety cell (specifically 4.5 million pigeon craps; 360,00 turkey craps; 45,000 emu craps), got five times as many retweets as the original post, and it got a lot of media attention as well. What's more, it showed that the car manufacturer has a great sense of humor and doesn't shy away from showing the brand's fun side. After all, everybody loves to laugh. And what people love more than a good laugh is the knowledge that brands have confidence in their products, which this funny infographic showed very clearly. Including the variety of bird species was also a nice touch.[4]

Well played, Smart Car. The brand's clever response was rewarded by the tweet you see on the right from Hove.

In the blog post, to which he linked in his response tweet, Hove called brand's response "INFOGRAPHANTASTIC." It isn't every day your brand's tweet inspires others to come up with the new word to describe it. Plus, Hove noted that this ingenious move by Smart Car made him rethink his perception of the brand. Not bad.

But is the smart social response all there is to real-time marketing, or is there something more?

Real-time marketing is no different from what good marketing has always been about—so why do we need a fancy new phrase for it?

> Real-time marketing goes to the heart of marketing: it is about raising awareness, creating demand, and furthering the brand's mission through connecting with customers in a meaningful way, in the right place, at the right time, through the relevant content.

> **Clayton Hove**
> @adtothebone
>
> Outsmarted by Smart Car
>
> adtothebone.com/?p=721
>
> Best. Social media response. Ever.
>
> ← Reply   ⇄ Retweet   ★ Favorite   ••• More
>
> **62**   **21**
> RETWEETS   FAVORITES
>
> 11:16 AM - 20 Jun 12

The Rise of Real-Time Marketing

Think of RTM and many people will cite the now-famous example of the Oreo tweet that went out during the 2013 Super Bowl XLVII blackout.

When America's biggest sporting event of the year was halted by a power outage that caused lights to go out for over half an hour, Oreo tweeted this spot-lit picture of a cookie with the caption, "You can still dunk in the dark." The tweet instantly went viral, with nearly 15,000 retweets and 20,000 likes on Facebook.[5] Oreo had captured a moment in cultural history and made it their own, to the delight of the millions of people who were sharing that moment on social media.

Though impressive, RTM has the potential to inform every part of a marketing strategy, not just grab headlines with clever comments and creative responses to current events. Too many brands are trying to replicate Oreo's success; the outpouring of material around the 2013 Academy Awards shows how many companies wanted to piggyback on the event's large Twitter audience, but most failed to understand what RTM is *really* about.

RTM is really not new at all. For as long as marketers have wanted to get the right message to the right person at the right time and place, there has been a need for a strategy capable of supporting this. What *is* new are the channels we have at our disposal to reach an unprecedented number of people and the data we have at our fingertips for an intelligent approach.

There is clearly a demand for a strategy that provides this intelligent approach. In a 2012 survey sponsored by Aprimo, a marketing automation software company, more than half (54%) of marketing professionals said that engaging their customers was a marketing challenge, and 52% cited the issue of competing for their customers' attention amid increasing noise.[6] Real-time marketing is a way for brands to cut through that noise and reach out to customers.

But we have to do it right. At one end of the spectrum are the brands initiating conversations and responding creatively to the zeitgeist—even informing it. At the other end are the companies who are more reminiscent of the school dork running around after the cool kids, eager to get his two cents in, trying way too hard.

So which one are you?

STATS

According to GolinHarris, there was a **14% increase** in the number of people who would try or buy from the brand, and an incredible **18% increase** following exposure to real-time marketing in the number of people who would recommend the brand to others.

It can be a fine line to tread, but getting it right can boost sales, bring new customers on board, and fuel peer-to-peer recommendations. The graph on the right by eMarketer, citing data from GolinHarris, shows the impact RTM can have on potential customers.[7] As you can see, positivity, interest, recommendations, consideration, and trying or buying of the brand were all markedly increased by exposure to real-time marketing.

We know that a marketer's goal is to get the right message to the right person at the right time and in the right place. But how do they know *who* is the right person, *when* is the right time, *which* is the right place, and *what* is the right message? That is where real-time listening and insights come in.

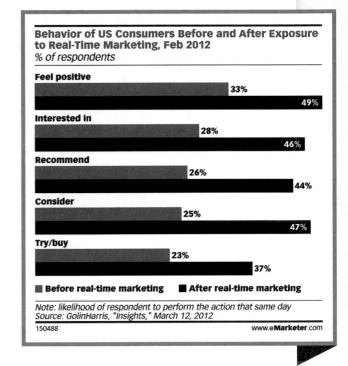

The 2013 eMarketer report *Meeting the Need for Speed: How Social Analytics Support Real-Time Marketing* breaks down the seven types of real-time marketing that exist, which gives an idea of the potential that exists for companies.

What is clear with RTM is that brands can't afford to ignore it in their marketing strategy. And 2013 appears to be the year that brands will have made the transition to using real-time data in their marketing campaigns. See the graph above from eMarketer, citing data from an Infogroup Targeting Solutions and Yesmail Interactive survey, for an overview of how brands are using real-time data.

So what is different now, and why is RTM suddenly an option for so many brands that may have overlooked it before?

To answer that, we need to look at how the resources available to marketers have changed as social media technology has moved from being an interesting sideline in a company's communications to being probably the most powerful tool available in the modern marketing tool box.

The Seven Types of Real-Time Marketing

1. **Real-time buying (RTB).** An automated method of buying and selling ad impressions on demand and on an impression-by-impression basis; often referred to as *programmatic buying*

2. **Dynamic creative optimization.** A method of automatically changing an ad's creatives to gain the best response from the ad's target audience

3. **Social customer relationship management (CRM).** A way of using social media to rapidly respond to customers who comment or complain on social media sites

4. **Real-time content marketing.** Using insights from social analytics to quickly develop digital content that meets an immediate marketing need

5. **Real-time ad campaign rebalancing.** Using insights gleaned from online conversations about ad campaigns to make on-the-fly changes in media mix or creatives

6. **Aligning marketing with trending topics.** Creating content, posts, or other marketing materials themed to news events or topics that social media users are discussing

7. **Strategic business decisions.** Applying insights from social media to rapidly make changes in product development, pricing, or other larger business activities[8]

Back in the 1960s advertising went through a revolution as television became ubiquitous in people's households. Think of *Mad Men*: stylish advertising executives telling people exactly what they needed and how a product would deliver the solution.

In the last few years marketing has gone through another revolution: the social revolution. Marketers no longer tell people what it is they want. Instead, they listen to customers' needs and develop products accordingly.

Successful marketing uses cutting-edge social technology to understand customers and anticipate need as never before. You bought a particular product? Here are two more suggestions based on your personal profile, tailored to your buying habits and network or friends. You are interested in an event? Here is how our brand is leading the conversation around that event. You have a comment, suggestion, or complaint? This is the creative response that will not only answer your query but will also turn you from a detractor to a committed fan, eager to tell your friends about our company.

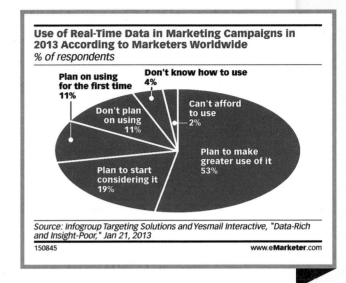

Real-time marketing is about more than a quick response. It is about creativity and driving dialogue, and about people doing real things and having meaningful conversations in real time. With so much social data at our fingertips, marketing departments can not only respond to the zeitgeist in real time but they can also drive it in a way that was unimaginable until now.

The availability of reliable, timely data has always been key to successful marketing campaigns, and the explosion of social media in the last five years has provided companies with a wealth of data—if they choose to make use of it.

You can see how RTM is about more than just advertising or smart content creation—it is about a relevant and timely two-way conversation between a brand and its customers. True RTM mentality needs to permeate all of the relevant internal stakeholders and strategies from a company's creative to its social responses, to traditional media and beyond. This is marketing at its very best.

STATS

Over half (**53%**) of brands surveyed were planning to make greater use of real-time data, with only **17%** of brands saying they either didn't plan on using it, didn't know how to, or couldn't afford to. First-time users numbered **11%**, a sizable adoption figure.[9]

> Great marketing is now a conversation based around communities and passions—and it needs to be flexible, responsive, and creative as never before.

The Importance of Agile Marketing and Social Data

Two things we can take away from Oreo's ability to produce clever content around current events are *relevance* and *creativity*.

But a good RTM strategy doesn't have to mean a constant rush to produce content in response to events. That can give a negative, knee-jerk appearance to your marketing. The best strategies mix real-time marketing into a carefully planned media campaign schedule. This means that RTM techniques can be used to tweak a campaign either in response to a changing mood before it is aired or as the campaign progresses by monitoring the public's reception to it. The audience will very likely never realize this more subtle approach is even happening, but timeliness, speed, and creativity will be just as important.

Real-time marketing content should support the wider marketing strategies of the brand, perhaps continuing a theme that has been prominent in its advertising, or it should encourage conversations around the new product lines or, better yet, the customers' needs. Departments need to be agile enough to react to situations that call for good, creative content, but they should not neglect their priorities in order to join in every conversation. It is easy to be overwhelmed by the amount of social data out there, but good agile marketing works when departments remain focused on their priorities. Companies shouldn't let their marketing strategy be swamped by gimmicky reactions to events, but good structuring can enable RTM to align with wider campaigns and to become a habit, or a way of life, in the day-to-day operation of brand marketers.

Marketing departments have had to change the way they operate in order to meet the challenges and opportunities that the availability of social data means for them. Social media command centers, pioneered by companies such as Cisco, Gatorade, and Dell, have become the norm in some larger organizations, and analytics tools have made the work of filtering data more effective. Companies have had to restructure the way decisions are made, and they have streamlined the processes by which content is generated and published.

"We can now do things far more swiftly and efficiently than we could before," says Grant Hunter, regional creative director for Asia-Pacific at iris Worldwide. "From a creative standpoint we have an arsenal of digital tools that allow us to stay up all night to code and design a microsite or generate amazing video content in a 24- to 48-hour window, or within minutes generate a Photoshop comp and then post it on Facebook."[10]

But in a June 2012 survey conducted by Stanford University, nearly two-thirds of senior executives said they did not use social media information to track the success of their business, and in a September 2012 study, Adobe found that two-thirds of marketers thought social media should be more "rooted in data," but fewer than 25% actually used social data for their marketing activities.[11]

To meet the goal of creative, timely, and relevant responses, brands must make use of the data available, and they must design everything from the structure of their marketing departments to the decision-making processes around the concept of agility.

Relevancy Has a Deadline— but Real-Time Marketing Takes Preparation

Images and videos are creative responses to events; they build on the zeitgeist rather than just giving an opinion, as a simple tweet might. They are easily shareable, and they resonate well with audiences, who appreciate original content. An image can also fit in well with corporate branding, being themed with the brand's color scheme, logos, or mascots. This means that no matter how widely the image is shared, it is still instantly recognizable as belonging to that brand.

> Brands can't simply become "more relevant" by commenting on the zeitgeist—not when everyone else is doing the same.
>
> **—IAN SCHAFER,** CEO of Deep Focus[12]

Timing is critical to creating responses in real time. For brands that are more used to organizing campaigns around the print ad and TV commercial, planned months in advance, the concept of turning around visuals in days or even hours can be hard to adapt to. But if your brand has a strong sense of the story it wants to tell, there's no reason why you can't integrate news items and cultural events that are relevant to your brand and give your brand's perspective on them through visual media. Not all brands need to turn images around quite as quickly as Oreo; some will have longer to respond depending on their audience and the news item. This fast turnaround means that brands have become more like publishers, thinking and operating in ways that enable them to give their take on relevant events on a rolling basis, as they happen.

It can help to think of these sorts of images as subplots to your main print and TV ads. You don't have to come up with whole new concepts. Once these have been agreed on, you can have more flexibility to adapt them to what it happening in the world around you in real time.

Without giving too much text explanation, companies can give their take on a whole range of situations with a well-developed image. Below are just some of the examples:

Real-Time Marketing Examples

1. **Twitter trending topics.** When the same-sex marriage bill passed in the United Kingdom recently, Virgin Holidays made sure they were part of the celebrations—and the company got in a timely reminder of their honeymoon packages at the same time.[13] The image read: "Same sex marriage bill passed. Time for a honeymoon." The text was accompanied by the visual of two full champagne glasses next to each other with each one showcasing a trace of red lipstick.

2. **Big events like the Super Bowl or the Olympics.** Oreo was the social media winner at the Super Bowl with its "You can still dunk in the dark" tweet—and it continued the theme at the Oscars, tweeting its own tribute to James Bond during a segment honoring the world's most famous secret agent.[14]

Real-Time Marketing Examples, *continued*

3. **Holidays or festivals.** General Electric celebrated February 11, Thomas Edison's birthday and Inventors' Day, by highlighting inventions and inventors and asking its audience to join in.[15]

4. **Current events such as a snowstorm, celebrity wedding, or royal baby.** Mini Cooper responded to a snowstorm by putting out an ad showing how its new all-wheel-drive Nemo model would help you "just keep swimming." The text accompanying the image of the car driving in the snow read: "Find your way through the storm." It was a timely and smart continuation of its existing marketing.

5. **Responding to a comment, criticism, or suggestion.** Some of the most creative visual responses have come from customer complaints. Bodyform recently released a video in reply to a humorous rant on its Facebook page by a man named Richard Neill, which took issue with Bodyform's glamorization of "this time of joy and 'blue water' and wings." His tongue-in-cheek complaint said that, as a man, he had been a little jealous of women's menstrual cycles, as portrayed by Bodyform. He said he had been delighted when he first got a girlfriend and "couldn't wait for this joyous adventurous time of the month to happen," but his anticipation soon turned to disbelief "as my lady changed from the loving, gentle, normal skin colored lady to the little girl from *The Exorcist* with added venom and extra 360-degree head spin." Bodyform had lied! Richard wanted to ask why Bodyform had misled men all these years through their advertising and why they had set him up for such a fall.

Over 100,000 people have now liked Richard's post. Bodyform's real-time mock-serious video reply featured CEO Caroline Williams (in reality an actress) pouring herself a glass of blue water and apologizing about the fact that the company had lied in its ads. Their adverts weren't, she explained, "a factual representation of events. . . . They are actually metaphors. They are not real. . . . There is no such thing as a happy period. . . . Some people simply can't handle the truth." Williams explained how the company's advertising hoped to shield men from the awful truth of what actually happens: "the mood swings, the cramps, the insatiable hunger, and—yes, Richard—the blood coursing from our uteri like a crimson landslide." But, she said, Richard's Facebook post had now "exposed all men to a reality we hoped they would never have to face." The video is hilarious and has now had over 5 million views. If you haven't seen it, you can watch it here:

(continued)

Real-Time Marketing Examples, *continued*

http://www.youtube.com/watch?v=Bpy75q 2DDow.[16]

6. **Latest craze, such as a viral YouTube video.** When it comes to responding to viral crazes, you really want to be among the first to add your own interpretation and not the hundredth. Because relevancy has a deadline. But there have been some inspired responses, such as Sony's *Cloudy with a Chance of Meatballs 2* viral trailer version of the Harlem Shake, an Internet meme featuring a 30-second dance, in which one person dances wildly unnoticed in a crowd until the bass drops and everyone else starts to dance, dressed in crazy outfits. Thousands of versions of the Harlem Shake were uploaded in early 2013, including ones by the Norwegian Army, football players from Manchester City, and the staff of *The Daily Show*.

Ekaterina participated in Intel's version of the Harlem Shake performed by Intel employees near Intel's Santa Clara campus. It was an off-the-cuff idea by Intel employees who brought funny costumes to campus to re-create their own fun version of the original video. Not only did it facilitate team building and make for a fun-filled lunch hour but also, much to the team's pleasant surprise, the video received over 120,000 organic views. The video not only showed the creativity of socially savvy Intel employees but it also allowed customers a glimpse inside the culture of a technology giant. You can watch Harlem Shake (Intel Edition) video here: http://www.youtube.com/watch?v=tjXxzvvGyyc.

It is important to remember that some of the best off-the-cuff photos and videos take preparation. Responding to a sporting event or to the Academy Awards can be preplanned (you know the day it will happen, and you can have several alternatives lined up ready to go whatever the outcome), but true real-time response requires you to develop the right internal infrastructure as well as a strong muscle memory. RTM is all about internal empowerment and practice.

Many brands have tried to emulate Oreo's successful Super Bowl tweet, but it was no "happy accident" or lucky event that can be copied by releasing a single image. Oreo had spent months building up its online audience and its RTM memory muscle through the clever use of RTM, such as the 100-day Daily Twist celebration. Oreo's marketing team had "trained" for the Super Bowl event by refining their real-time creative response process and incorporating it into their day-to-day routine, much as an athlete would train for a big event.

There is a difference between planning and preparation. The Oreo team had prepared for an event such as the Super Bowl blackout (which no one could predict) through months of trial and improvement of their real-time response technique. That was why their "You can still dunk in the dark" image tweet was so successful: behind the glib message were months of hard work and practice for that moment.

The Oreo team's example is great because it shows how the RTM response process needs to be ingrained in the everyday running of a brand's marketing. There will be many days when there is no cultural event that particularly resonates with a brand's audience or with its core message, but when an Internet meme, a topical news story, or a customer comment does occur that resonates particularly well, the brand is poised and ready to respond in an original, well-thought-out, and creative way.

> Relevancy has a deadline.

When real-time marketing is done well, it can make for a brand that understands its customers, reflects their needs in product designs, deals sensitively with feedback, and drives the conversation around its expertise. The obvious problems with RTM are that it can be a highly visible method of marketing and the structure has to be in place within an organization to support the information flow into and out of the marketing department.

We know that for successful RTM, agility is everything. Agility doesn't have to mean that you are able to respond to every event instantly; that could lead to knee-jerk reactions and a fragmented approach to your overall marketing strategy. But organizational structures, particularly for the largest brands, can be large and inflexible, and processes can be slow. Marketing departments are used to planning months ahead, with much research and testing before campaigns get the go-ahead. RTM demands a more flexible approach, often with more autonomy than these departments are used to.

Even if a brand's products are not suited to on-the-fly promotion or quick responses (for example, many companies in highly regulated industries have heavy involvement from the legal team before anything can be released), RTM can still be used to monitor responses, gauge customer involvement, or provide market research. If you think past the more headline-grabbing examples and you look into how data and analytics can work for you, you may find that there are many ways you can make use of the insights they provide.

Obviously, RTM gone wrong can lead to negative buzz. There have been some notable tweets or Facebook posts in response to events that have been in particularly bad taste. Kenneth Cole famously made a joke at the expense of the violent Cairo uprisings, and the food website *Epicurious* sent out a tweet that seemed to make light of the Boston bombings. The marketers behind them had jumped on the RTM bandwagon too eagerly. There is a time and a place for promotion, and this wasn't the time or the place.

Some companies' unfortunately prescheduled tweets have caused customers' indignation. News of supermarket giant Tesco's involvement in the horsemeat scandal had just broken when this tweet came from its account: "It's sleepy time so we're off to hit the hay! See you at 8 a.m. for more #TescoTweets." There was public outrage at what looked like a horse-related pun at a time when the company's customers were shocked that they may have eaten contaminated meat. Tesco quickly apologized, saying that the "tweet was scheduled before we knew of the current situation."[17]

Real-time marketing is not just about composing messages. It is also about monitoring output as it relates to the public mood. In the examples just cited, a more receptive strategy would have made sure that future tweets were filtered against social and topical information *before* they went out, which would have prevented an embarrassing situation.

Not all RTM social media fails have been quite so badly judged. Sometimes coming across as unoriginal or tacky can be detrimental to a brand too. If your definition of real-time marketing means solely commenting on current events or riding the wave of a trending topic, then you're just adding another voice to the noise. The reaction of many people to brands' output around the 2013 Academy Awards was that they had mostly missed an opportunity for a creative response. You don't want to be the last on the bandwagon, but as a marketer, you also want to make sure your marketing content is relevant to the situation, that it builds on your overall marketing strategy, and that it is consistent with your brand's purpose and voice.

The Future: Four-Dimesional Marketing

Real-time marketing is in its infancy. The near-ubiquitous presence of smartphones makes for an extra dimension to RTM: that of geolocation. Imagine if you could add on-the-go geographical information to your RTM stats. You could anticipate how the customers' needs change as they move through their day—which restaurant to recommend based on their profile; which advertising will resonate with them at this moment in time (there is no point in showing an advert for winter clothing to a New Yorker on vacation in Florida); and where their friends are right now.

But before we can get there, we need to work on the way we structure our marketing departments to support making RTM a mentality, making it central to the way we approach various aspects of marketing. Research, development, strategies, customer service, execution of campaign, and conversing on relevant topics can all be underpinned by real-time marketing strategies. That way we can be agile and face the future with the right knowledge and tools at our fingertips.

To succeed with real-time marketing, we have to change our understanding of the basics of *how* we market, from the way we organize to the way we think. We need to bring the essential departments together—creative, analytics, paid media, social media, legal, and strategic—so that we can work in a time-critical way. With the foundations in place, we can make sure that the marketing direction is tightly aligned with stakeholders so that RTM supports the direction of the brand now and into the future. With the right mentality we can use the considerable tools and data at our disposal to streamline the creative process and make it responsive to cultural events and customer interests. We need to be prepared and poised so that when the right moment comes, we can take hold of it and make it our own.

Real-time marketing can help tell a brand's visual story if we are trained to tell that story as part of our everyday marketing strategy. We need to be clear on which events are relevant to our brand and our customers. Then we can create visuals that show our brand's perspective on those events, in effect to use them as props in our story. This brings our brand's story to life and gives it an everyday relevance.

Conclusion

T here's no doubt that this is an exciting time for brands and consumers alike. We're doing business in an era when disruption is celebrated and consumers are savvier than ever before. Phrases like "innovate or die" have become the norm, pushing marketers to work smarter and inviting them to break through the clutter to tell their brand story.

The proliferation of social media platforms, with sizeable followings to match, has resulted in an increased focus on maximizing the potential of these communities. Successful marketers have realized that these sites have become increasingly visual—and not just by choice. Changing consumer behavior, as well as demand to see and share visuals and rich media, is driving both consumption and engagement.

Visit any social media platform on a given day and you'll find a never-ending stream of visual content. In the age of "infobesity" and increasing digital noise, visual storytelling has emerged as a strategy for not only standing out, but also for nurturing and growing vibrant and engaged communities. The ability to craft visuals that inspire emotion and action is helping companies to be noticed and is amplifying their stories through those communities. Consumers don't necessarily go to social media sites to hear from companies, but a compelling visual can pull them into an intriguing story or provide a valuable lesson, resulting in increased brand awareness, loyalty, a desired action, or even sales.

To master visual storytelling, you need a powerful toolkit at your disposal. With this book, we wanted to share strategy, resources, and other tools to set you up for success in not only building a case for a powerful content strategy, but also in crafting your company's visual story. It's our hope that this book will also serve as a creative catalyst, inspiring you to test and innovate different approaches to visual storytelling.

Although it's hard to say what's next when it comes to the social and digital revolution, there is one thing we can all agree on. Visuals and rich media will continue to play an important role in the way we create, consume, and distribute information. Understanding how consumers prefer to receive information and how those preferences evolve over time is key to sustainable marketing and business success.

Change is no longer an *if* in the digital and social media world, it's a *when*. Ensuring that you are ready to react to change will guarantee that your visual story doesn't just have a beginning, middle, and end, but that it also has a series of plot twists that will inspire your customers and keep them coming back for more.

Are you ready to start telling *your* visual story?

SURPRISING
USER-GENERATED
EXPERIMENTAL
INTERACTIVE CURATED
SHARE-WORTHY
MOTIVATIONAL
POWERFUL STORYTELLING TRUSTED
VALUE-ADD INSPIRATIONAL
CAPTIVATING EDUCATIONAL
REAL-TIME EMOTIONAL COLORFUL
RELEVANT
AUTHENTIC
DESIGN

Design by Eric Egerton

Acknowledgments

First and foremost, we would like to thank you, the reader, for picking up our book. Writing this book has very much been a passion project for us both, and we hope that you found everything you were looking for inside.

We would like to offer our deepest gratitude to the marketers who contributed their inspiration and encouragement to this book, including, but not limited to Jay Baer, Laura Fitton, Dan Roam, Brian Solis, Jennifer Lashua, Bryan Rhoads, Wendy Lea, Tom Fishburne, Claudia Allwood, and Debra Aho Williamson.

A special acknowledgment goes to Steve Garfield, a friend and amazing visual storyteller in his own right, for taking such a lovely headshot of us for the book. We would also like to thank Jennifer Stakes Roberts for her unparalleled support on this project.

It has been a gratifying experience to work with the fantastic team at McGraw-Hill, who have been with us every step of the way. The content and the drastically different visual format are a testament to the team and their commitment to innovative publishing.

Most importantly, we are thankful to our friends and family who encouraged and supported us along the way. You are a gift! Our accomplishments are your accomplishments.

Last, but certainly not least, this book is a testament to the value of relationship building and how amazing opportunities come to you when you least expect it. Although we had known each other for some time through the social media industry, spending several days together at LeWeb 2012 in Paris was truly a catalyst in developing the concept for this book. We would like to thank our friends from LeWeb Paris—Cédric Giorgi, Loïc, and Geraldine Le Meur—for serendipitously bringing us together on this project.

As you close this final page of this book energized to leverage the power of visual storytelling, remember the work that you do is just as important as the relationships you build.

Ekaterina and Jessica

Notes

Introduction

1. http://www.goodreads.com/author/quotes/3503.Maya_Angelou.

Chapter 1

1. http://www.socialmediaexaminer.com/storytelling-with-images/.
2. http://moz.com/ugc/brands-take-to-instagram-for-marketing.
3. http://www.youtube.com/yt/press/statistics.html.
4. http://www.business2community.com/social-media/3-shocking-social-media-stats
   -that-will-amp-up-your-marketing-0264544#LWR5SBCcHLobR3SV.99.
5. http://venturebeat.com/2013/02/27/sephora-our-pinterest-followers-spend-15x-more
   -than-our-facebook-followers/.
6. https://www.facebook.com/blog/blog.php?post=2207967130.
7. http://www.insidefacebook.com/2007/12/18/top-10-facebook-stories-of-2007/.
8. http://www.insidefacebook.com/2007/12/18/top-10-facebook-stories-of-2007/.
9. http://www.insidefacebook.com/2007/12/09/inside-facebook-marketing-bible-24
   -ways-to-market-your-brand-company-product-or-service-in-facebook/.
10. http://www.socialmediaexplorer.com/social-media-marketing/facebook-group-and
    -brand-page-best-practices/.
11. http://simplymeasured.com/blog/2012/03/27/the-impact-of-facebook-timeline-for
    -brands-study/.
12. http://mashable.com/2013/03/07/new-facebook-news-feed/.
13. Ekaterina Walter, *Think Like Zuck,* McGraw-Hill, 2013.
14. http://www.socialmediaexaminer.com/storytelling-with-images/.

15. http://mobithinking.com/mobile-marketing-tools/latest-mobile-stats/a#subscribers.
16. http://library.thinkquest.org/08aug/00869/whendidlanguagestart.html.
17. From http://www.b2bcontentengine.com/2012/08/09/19-reasons-you-should-include-visual-content-in-your-marketing-data/, based on research from http://www.billiondollargraphics.com/infographics.html and http://www.webmarketinggroup.co.uk/Blog/why-every-seo-strategy-needs-infographics-1764.aspx.
18. http://www.businessballs.com/mehrabiancommunications.htm.
19. From http://www.b2bcontentengine.com/2012/08/09/19-reasons-you-should-include-visual-content-in-your-marketing-data/, based on research from http://www.billiondollargraphics.com/infographics.html.
20. From http://heidicohen.com/5-facts-prove-visual-content-is-a-guaranteed-winner/, based on research from http://www.mdgadvertising.com/blog/its-all-about-the-images-infographic/.
21. http://paulbiedermann.sharedby.co/share/oP1Q4H.
22. http://resources.bazaarvoice.com/rs/bazaarvoice/images/201202_Millennials_whitepaper.pdf.
23. http://www.mediabistro.com/alltwitter/91-of-b2b-marketers-now-use-social-media-for-content-marketing-study_b44220.
24. From http://www.b2bcontentengine.com/2012/08/09/19-reasons-you-should-include-visual-content-in-your-marketing-data/, based on research from http://www.billiondollargraphics.com/infographics.html and http://www.webmarketinggroup.co.uk/Blog/why-every-seo-strategy-needs-infographics-1764.aspx.
25. From http://www.b2bcontentengine.com/2012/08/09/19-reasons-you-should-include-visual-content-in-your-marketing-data/, based on research from http://www.webmarketinggroup.co.uk/Blog/why-every-seo-strategy-needs-infographics-1764.aspx.
26. http://mashable.com/2013/04/29/snackable-content-buzzword/.
27. http://www.comscore.com/Insights/Blog/2013_Digital_Future_in_Focus_Series.
28. From http://heidicohen.com/5-facts-prove-visual-content-is-a-guaranteed-winner/, based on research from http://www.mdgadvertising.com/blog/its-all-about-the-images-infographic/.
29. From http://heidicohen.com/5-facts-prove-visual-content-is-a-guaranteed-winner/, based on research from http://www.mdgadvertising.com/blog/its-all-about-the-images-infographic/.
30. http://mashable.com/2013/04/25/nestivity-engaged-brands.
31. http://www.customcontentcouncil.com/news/nearly-44-billion-new-survey-shows-rise-content-marketing-budget.
32. From http://heidicohen.com/5-facts-prove-visual-content-is-a-guaranteed-winner/, based on research from http://www.mdgadvertising.com/blog/its-all-about-the-images-infographic/.
33. From http://heidicohen.com/5-facts-prove-visual-content-is-a-guaranteed-winner/, based on research from http://www.mdgadvertising.com/blog/its-all-about-the-images-infographic/.

34. From http://www.b2bcontentengine.com/2012/08/09/19-reasons-you-should-include -visual-content-in-your-marketing-data/, based on research from http://www.billion dollargraphics.com/infographics.html.

35. From http://www.b2bcontentengine.com/2012/08/09/19-reasons-you-should-include -visual-content-in-your-marketing-data/, based on research from http://ansonalex .com/infographics/infographic-effectiveness-statistics-infographic/.

36. From http://www.b2bcontentengine.com/2012/08/09/19-reasons-you-should-include -visual-content-in-your-marketing-data/, based on research from http://moz.com/ blog/what-makes-a-link-worthy-post-part-1.

37. http://www.marketingsherpa.com/article/how-to/videos-attract-300-more-traffic.

38. http://www.location3.com/why-visual-content-is-essential/.

39. http://www.jeffbullas.com/2012/05/28/6-powerful-reasons-why-you-should-include -images-in-your-marketing-infographic/#Rqga52Olcrs0z5oL.99.

40. http://www.jeffbullas.com/2012/05/28/6-powerful-reasons-why-you-should-include -images-in-your-marketing-infographic/.

41. http://www.jeffbullas.com/2012/05/28/6-powerful-reasons-why-you-should-include -images-in-your-marketing-infographic/.

42. http://www.jeffbullas.com/2012/05/28/6-powerful-reasons-why-you-should-include -images-in-your-marketing-infographic/.

43. http://www.jeffbullas.com/2012/05/28/6-powerful-reasons-why-you-should-include -images-in-your-marketing-infographic/.

44. http://www.jeffbullas.com/2012/05/28/6-powerful-reasons-why-you-should-include -images-in-your-marketing-infographic/.

45. http://www.eyeviewdigital.com/documents/eyeview_brochure.pdf.

Chapter 2

1. http://www.brainyquote.com/quotes/keywords/pictures_2. html#Ic00mwK601F8eQG0.99.

2. http://mashable.com/2013/05/29/mary-meeker-internet-trends-2013/.

3. http://www.urbandictionary.com/define.php?term=pics%20or%20it%20didn't%20 happen.

4. Richard Dawkins, *The Selfish Gene,* 30th anniversary ed., Oxford University Press USA, New York, 1976.

5. http://www.amusingplanet.com/2013/06/lolcats-from-yesteryears-photographs-by .html.

6. http://www.brandchannel.com/home/post/Home-Depot-Richard-Meme-041913 .aspx.

7. http://mwpdigitalmedia.com/blog/why-web-video-should-be-central-to-your-social -media-strategy/.

8. http://www.prdaily.com/Main/Articles/14623.aspx#.

9. http://www.jeffbullas.com/2012/04/23/48-significant-social-media-facts-figures-and
-statistics-plus-7-infographics/#eH2WSfuoRDRMslUy.99.

10. http://mashable.com/2013/05/15/viral-video-factors/.

11. http://brandongaille.com/slideshare-statistics-and-marketing-tips/.

12. http://brandongaille.com/slideshare-statistics-and-marketing-tips/.

13. http://www.ragan.com/Main/Articles/5_ways_Whole_Foods_builds_awareness_
on_Pinterest_46293.aspx.

14. http://online.wsj.com/article/SB10001424127887324216004578483094260521704
.html.

15. http://postcards.blogs.fortune.cnn.com/2012/10/17/coke-clark-facebook/.

16. http://postcards.blogs.fortune.cnn.com/2012/10/17/coke-clark-facebook/.

17. http://www.buzzfeed.com/andrewgauthier/the-incredible-amount-of-stuff-that
-happens-on-the-internet.

Chapter 3

1. From http://www.b2bcontentengine.com/2012/08/09/19-reasons-you-should-include
-visual-content-in-your-marketing-data/, based on research from http://www.billion
dollargraphics.com/infographics.html and http://www.webmarketinggroup.co.uk/
Blog/why-every-seo-strategy-needs-infographics-1764.aspx.

2. http://mashable.com/2013/04/29/snackable-content-buzzword/.

3. http://blog.shareaholic.com/2012/01/pinterest-referral-traffic.

4. http://sherpablog.marketingsherpa.com/b2b-marketing/channel-marketing/b2b
-pinterest-content-marketing/.

5. http://sherpablog.marketingsherpa.com/b2b-marketing/channel-marketing/b2b
-pinterest-content-marketing/.

6. http://www.fastcompany.com/3008342/what-pinterest-redesign-means-brands.

7. http://www.searchenginejournal.com/pinterestingly-enough-interesting-pinterest
-stats/45328/.

8. http://www.businessinsider.com/pinterest-is-worth-2-billion-because-its-25-million
-users-are-rich-female-and-like-to-spend-2013-2.

9. http://venturebeat.com/2013/02/27/sephora-our-pinterest-followers-spend-15x-more
-than-our-facebook-followers/.

10. http://new.pitchengine.com/pitches/0b0228ae-1ace-4f56-8c50-3cdef44d88b1.

11. http://new.pitchengine.com/pitches/0b0228ae-1ace-4f56-8c50-3cdef44d88b1.

12. http://new.pitchengine.com/pitches/0b0228ae-1ace-4f56-8c50-3cdef44d88b1.

13. http://www.shop.org/c/journal_articles/view_article_content?groupId=1&article
Id=1541&version=1.0.

14. http://www.shopify.com/blog/6058268-how-pinterest-drives-ecommerce-sales#axzz
2SEv3Ya59.

15. http://www.nielsen.com/us/en/newswire/2012/digital-lives-of-american-moms.html.

16. http://www.blogher.com/women-and-social-media-2012.

17. http://www.richrelevance.com/.
18. http://www.mediabistro.com/alltwitter/social-media-stats-2012_b30651.
19. http://www.arikhanson.com/2012/02/21/18-compelling-stats-to-help-sell-your-boss -on-pinterest/.
20. http://blog.curalate.com/pinterest-85-percent-organic/.
21. http://www.repinly.com/stats.aspx.
22. https://blog.compete.com/2012/06/28/pinning-down-the-impact-of-pinterest/.
23. http://blog.shareaholic.com/2012/01/pinterest-referral-traffic.
24. http://www.businessinsider.com/pinterest-is-worth-2-billion-because-its-25-million -users-are-rich-female-and-like-to-spend-2013-2#ixzz2UbNXVo00.
25. http://new.pitchengine.com/pitches/0b0228ae-1ace-4f56-8c50-3cdef44d88b1.
26. http://www.she-conomy.com/facts-on-women.
27. http://www.she-conomy.com/facts-on-women.
28. http://blog.hubspot.com/blog/tabid/6307/bid/33845/8-Real-Life-Examples-of -Engaging-Pinterest-Contests.aspx.
29. http://www.socialmediaexaminer.com/pinterest-contest/.
30. http://www.jeffbullas.com/2012/04/23/48-significant-social-media-facts-figures-and -statistics-plus-7-infographics/#eWSfuoRDRMslUy.99.
31. http://www.entrepreneur.com/article/226924.
32. http://www.jeffbullas.com/2012/04/23/48-significant-social-media-facts-figures-and -statistics-plus-7-infographics/#eWSfuoRDRMslUy.99.
33. http://www.changeboard.com/content/2854/bring-your-brand-to-life-through-the -power-of-video/.
34. http://www.changeboard.com/content/2854/bring-your-brand-to-life-through-the -power-of-video/.
35. http://www.jeffbullas.com/2012/04/23/48-significant-social-media-facts-figures-and -statistics-plus-7-infographics/#eWSfuoRDRMslUy.99.
36. http://www.jeffbullas.com/2012/04/23/48-significant-social-media-facts-figures-and -statistics-plus-7-infographics/#eWSfuoRDRMslUy.99.
37. http://www.jeffbullas.com/2012/04/23/48-significant-social-media-facts-figures-and -statistics-plus-7-infographics/#eWSfuoRDRMslUy.99.
38. http://www.youtube.com/yt/press/statistics.html.
39. http://www.youtube.com/yt/press/statistics.html.
40. http://www.youtube.com/yt/press/statistics.html.
41. http://www.youtube.com/yt/press/statistics.html.
42. http://www.youtube.com/yt/press/statistics.html.
43. http://www.jeffbullas.com/2012/04/23/48-significant-social-media-facts-figures-and -statistics-plus-7-infographics/#eWSfuoRDRMslUy.99.
44. http://www.youtube.com/yt/press/statistics.html.
45. http://www.youtube.com/yt/press/statistics.html.
46. http://www.youtube.com/yt/press/statistics.html.
47. http://www.clickz.com/clickz/news/2198728/video-drives-clothing-sales.

48. http://bespokevideoproduction.wordpress.com/2011/04/08/kiss-goodbye-to-the-30 -second-ad-youtube-branded-clips-and-click-to-buy-are-redefining-the-who-what -where-when-and-how-of-online-campaigns/.

49. http://www.nytimes.com/2013/04/11/business/smallbusiness/dollar-shave-club-from -viral-video-to-real-business.html?pagewanted=all&_r=1&.

50. http://www.forbes.com/sites/capitalonespark/2013/01/23/tell-dont-sell-use-content -marketing-to-boost-your-business.

51. http://blog.hubspot.com/blog/tabid/6307/bid/33629/50-of-Facebook-Fans-Prefer -Brand-Pages-to-Company-Websites-INFOGRAPHIC.aspx.

52. http://www.socialmediaexaminer.com/storytelling-with-images/.

53. http://simplymeasured.com/blog/2012/03/27/the-impact-of-facebook-timeline-for -brands-study/.

54. http://techcrunch.com/2013/01/17/facebook-photos-record/.

55. http://www.business2community.com/facebook/facebook-marketing-statistics-you -need-to-know-0289953.

56. http://www.business2community.com/facebook/facebook-marketing-statistics-you -need-to-know-0289953.

57. http://uberly.com/facebook-statistics-2012/.

58. http://offers.hubspot.com/2013-state-of-inbound-marketing?__hstc=20629287 .70b52168144dff23b49a5912d139749f.1370872534479.1370872534479.13708725344 79.1&__hssc=20629287.1.1370872534479.

59. http://offers.hubspot.com/2013-state-of-inbound-marketing?__hstc=20629287 .70b52168144dff23b49a5912d139749f.1370872534479.1370872534479.13708725 34479.1&__hssc=20629287.1.1370872534479.

60. http://www.syncapse.com/value-of-a-facebook-fan-2013/#.UW6uQrVJNQU.

61. http://www.experian.com/blogs/marketing-forward/2012/02/07/10-key-statistics -about-facebook/.

62. http://www.zdnet.com/blog/facebook/facebook-accounts-for-1-in-every-7-online -minutes/6639.

63. http://www.digiday.com/brands/10-stats-brands-should-know-about-facebook/.

64. There are 2.5 billion content shares a day on Facebook.

65. http://www.digiday.com/brands/10-stats-brands-should-know-about-facebook.

66. http://venturebeat.com/2013/03/05/facebook-15-million-businesses-companies-and -organizations-now-have-a-facebook-page.

67. http://www.slideshare.net/performics_us/performics-life-on-demand-2012 -summary-deck.

68. http://www.nytimes.com/2011/06/29/business/media/29adco.html?_r=0.

69. http://blog.neworld.com/2011/how-a-facebook-campaign-increased-sales-by-35-and -generated-pr-worth-200/.

70. http://www.businesswire.com/news/home/20130516005749/en/Harlem-Globetrotters -Increases-Web-Traffic-Geo-Targeted-Facebook.

71. http://cdn.pamorama.net/wp-content/uploads/2013/05/HubSpot-Facebook -marketing-case-study.pdf.

72. http://www.mediabistro.com/alltwitter/social-photo-video_b27506.
73. http://therealtimereport.com/2011/03/18/77-of-fortune-global-100-companies-use-twitter/.
74. http://therealtimereport.com/2011/03/18/77-of-fortune-global-100-companies-use-twitter/.
75. http://therealtimereport.com/2011/03/18/77-of-fortune-global-100-companies-use-twitter/.
76. http://therealtimereport.com/2011/03/18/77-of-fortune-global-100-companies-use-twitter/.
77. https://blog.twitter.com/2011/numbers.
78. https://blog.twitter.com/2011/numbers.
79. https://blog.twitter.com/2011/numbers.
80. https://blog.twitter.com/2011/numbers.
81. https://blog.twitter.com/2011/numbers.
82. http://www.sysomos.com/insidetwitter/mostactiveusers/.
83. http://www.sysomos.com/insidetwitter/mostactiveusers/.
84. http://offers.hubspot.com/how-to-use-twitter-for-business.
85. http://offers.hubspot.com/how-to-use-twitter-for-business.
86. http://www.socialtechnologyreview.com/articles/40-fascinating-twitter-facts.
87. http://mashable.com/2013/04/25/nestivity-engaged-brands.
88. http://www.digitalbuzzblog.com/volkswagen-fox-twitter-zoom-campaign.
89. http://socialmediatoday.com/bryannagy/1211641/coca-cola-s-twitter-contest-heart-truth.
90. http://www.prnewswire.com/news-releases/radioshack-campaign-honored-for-social-media-innovation-132789133.html.
91. http://mashable.com/2013/06/27/instagram-video-top-brands/.
92. http://mashable.com/2013/06/27/instagram-video-top-brands/.
93. http://www.newsreach.co.uk/knowledge-centre/news/social-media-marketing/instagram-me-happy-brands-turning-to-visual-marketing/.
94. http://online.wsj.com/article_email/SB10001424127887324577304579059230069305894-lMyQjAxMTAzMDAwODEwNDgyWj.html.
95. http://moz.com/ugc/brands-take-to-instagram-for-marketing.
96. http://www.forbes.com/sites/marketshare/2012/08/13/more-brands-joining-instagram-and-with-good-reason/.
97. http://appdata.com.
98. Simply Measured.
99. http://moz.com/ugc/brands-take-to-instagram-for-marketing.
100. http://moz.com/ugc/brands-take-to-instagram-for-marketing.
101. http://www.businessinsider.com/statistics-that-reveal-instagrams-mind-blowing-success-2012-4.
102. http://www.digitalbuzzblog.com/infographic-instagram-stats/.
103. http://moz.com/ugc/brands-take-to-instagram-for-marketing.
104. http://mashable.com/2012/10/09/instagram-felix-baumgartner-red-bull/.

105. http://mashable.com/2012/02/02/ford-fiesta-instagram/.
106. http://mashable.com/2012/02/02/ford-fiesta-instagram/.
107. http://www.clickz.com/clickz/column/2239636/tumblr-untapped-marketing -goldmine.
108. http://leaderswest.com/2013/06/13/infographic-average-time-per-visit-on-tumblr-is -34-minutes/.
109. http://dachisgroup.com/2013/04/no-comment-using-tumblr-to-tell-your-brand -story/.
110. http://leaderswest.com/2013/06/13/infographic-average-time-per-visit-on-tumblr-is -34-minutes/.
111. http://blogs.wsj.com/digits/2013/05/20/the-numbers-behind-tumblr/.
112. http://www.tumblr.com/about.
113. http://www.tumblr.com/about.
114. http://www.comscore.com/Insights/Blog.
115. http://www.comscore.com/Insights/Blog.
116. http://www.comscore.com/Insights/Blog.
117. http://leaderswest.com/2013/06/13/infographic-average-time-per-visit-on-tumblr-is -34-minutes/.
118. http://leaderswest.com/2013/06/13/infographic-average-time-per-visit-on-tumblr-is -34-minutes/.
119. http://www.brandchannel.com/home/post/Tumblr-Brand-Marketing-011412.aspx.
120. http://www.clickz.com/clickz/column/2239636/tumblr-untapped-marketing -goldmine.
121. http://www.clickz.com/clickz/column/2239636/tumblr-untapped-marketing -goldmine.
122. http://www.clickz.com/clickz/column/2239636/tumblr-untapped-marketing -goldmine.
123. http://www.clickz.com/clickz/column/2239636/tumblr-untapped-marketing -goldmine.
124. http://repcapitalmedia.com/public-sector-case-study-the-world-bank-wows-fans -with-tumblr/.
125. http://industry.shortyawards.com/category/4th_annual/tumblr_brand/RO/ happiness-is-coca-cola-on-tumblr.
126. http://socialmediatoday.com/brett-williams/1017741/best-times-post-tumblr.
127. http://industry.shortyawards.com/nominee/4th_annual/YI/doctor-who-tumblr.
128. http://adage.com/article/digital/tumblr-unveils-major-brand-campaign -adidas/235262/.
129. http://www.ignitesocialmedia.com/video-marketing/brand-on-vine/.
130. http://www.name.com/blog/general/2013/06/how-to-use-vine-to-extend-your -brands-social-media-reach/.
131. http://www.ignitesocialmedia.com/video-marketing/brand-on-vine/.
132. http://www.unrulymedia.com/article/08-05-2013/unruly-unveils-top-vine-metrics -and-100-most-tweeted-vines-celebrate-app%E2%80%99s-100-da.

133. http://www.ignitesocialmedia.com/video-marketing/brand-on-vine/.
134. http://www.unrulymedia.com/article/08-05-2013/unruly-unveils-top-vine-metrics -and-100-most-tweeted-vines-celebrate-app%E2%80%99s-100-da.
135. http://www.ignitesocialmedia.com/video-marketing/brand-on-vine/.
136. http://www.unrulymedia.com/article/08-05-2013/unruly-unveils-top-vine-metrics -and-100-most-tweeted-vines-celebrate-app%E2%80%99s-100-da.
137. http://socialmediatoday.com/julie-blakley/1516266/7-brands-getting-creative-vine.
138. http://socialmediatoday.com/julie-blakley/1516266/7-brands-getting-creative-vine.
139. . http://www.ignitesocialmedia.com/video-marketing/brand-on-vine/ http://www .clickz.com/clickz/news/2268718/dunkin-donuts-hops-on-twitters-vine-for-latest -campaign.
140. http://blog.hubspot.com/blog/tabid/6307/bid/34144/How-15-Real-Businesses-Are -Getting-Creative-With-Vine-for-Marketing.aspx.
141. http://www.name.com/blog/general/2013/06/how-to-use-vine-to-extend-your -brands-social-media-reach/.
142. http://blog.hubspot.com/blog/tabid/6307/bid/34144/How-15-Real-Businesses-Are -Getting-Creative-With-Vine-for-Marketing.aspx.
143. http://www.slideshare.net/about.
144. http://www.slideshare.net/about.
145. http://brandongaille.com/slideshare-statistics-and-marketing-tips/.
146. http://brandongaille.com/slideshare-statistics-and-marketing-tips/.
147. http://brandongaille.com/slideshare-statistics-and-marketing-tips/.
148. http://www.slideshare.net/slidesharepro/10m-infographic.
149. http://brandongaille.com/slideshare-statistics-and-marketing-tips/.
150. http://contentmarketinginstitute.com/education/books/the-marketers-guide-to -slideshare/.
151. http://techcrunch.com/2012/01/17/techcrunch-readers-love-slideshare/.
152. http://www.slideshare.net/about.
153. http://www.forbes.com/sites/marketshare/2013/02/28/slideshare-the-quiet-giant-of -content-marketing/.
154. http://blog.slideshare.net/2011/10/12/guest-post-karen-leland-use-slideshare-to-tell -your-small-business-story/.
155. http://blog.slideshare.net/2013/06/04/how-achievers-leveraged-slideshare-and -linkedin-to-increase-lead-gens/.
156. http://blog.slideshare.net/2012/04/30/salesforce-casting-a-wider-net-via-the-social -web-2/.
157. http://www.business2community.com/google-plus/getting-started-with-google-plus -marketing-0508915.
158. http://www.searchenginejournal.com/google-plus-surpasses-twitter-to-become -second-largest-social-network/57740/.
159. http://searchengineland.com/google-worlds-most-popular-search-engine-148089.
160. http://socialfresh.com/seriously-who-is-using-google-plus-and-why/.
161. http://socialfresh.com/seriously-who-is-using-google-plus-and-why/.

162. http://techsavvynyc.com/google-plus-demographics/.
163. http://techsavvynyc.com/google-plus-demographics/.
164. http://techsavvynyc.com/google-plus-demographics/.
165. http://www.clickz.com/clickz/column/2250858/small-businesses-are-benefiting -from-google-presence.
166. http://en.community.dell.com/dell-groups/sbc/b/weblog/archive/2013/05/20/trey -ratcliff-s-google-domination-visual-content-tips-for-marketers.aspx.
167. http://www.google.co.uk/think/case-studies/cadbury-sweet-google-plus.html.

Chapter 4

1. http://www.andreavahl.com/social-media/29-of-the-best-social-media-quotes.php.
2. http://burberry.tumblr.com.
3. http://businesstoday.intoday.in/story/burberry-social-media-initiative/1/191422 .html.
4. Jonah Peretti, Keynote Speech, SXSW 2013.
5. http://www.youtube.com/watch?v=T6MhAwQ64c0.

Chapter 5

1. http://theinspirationroom.com/daily/2013/oreo-daily-twist/.
2. http://dachisgroup.com/2013/06/real-time-marketing-definition/.
3. http://www.emarketer.com/Article/Originality-Content-Marketers-Greatest -Challenge/1009495.
4. http://www.zdnet.com/blog/feeds/smart-usa-does-the-math-on-twitter-about -pigeon-crap/4921.
5. http://www.wired.com/underwire/2013/02/oreo-twitter-super-bowl/.
6. eMarketer, Inc., *Meeting the Need for Speed: How Social Analytics Support Real-Time Marketing*, February 2013, p. 2.
7. http://www.emarketer.com/Article/Real-Time-Marketing-Drumbeat-Gets-Louder -Agencies-Brands-Sign-On/1009869.
8. eMarketer, Inc., *Meeting the Need for Speed: How Social Analytics Support Real-Time Marketing*, February 2013, p. 2.
9. eMarketer, Inc., *Meeting the Need for Speed: How Social Analytics Support Real-Time Marketing*, February 2013, p. 5.
10. http://www.emarketer.com/Article/Real-Time-Marketing-Drumbeat-Gets-Louder -Agencies-Brands-Sign-On/1009869.
11. eMarketer, Inc. *Meeting the Need for Speed: How Social Analytics Support Real-Time Marketing*, February 2013, p. 9.
12. http://adage.com/article/guest-columnists/fast-truths-real-time-marketing/239959/.
13. http://www.toprankblog.com/2013/04/real-time-marketing-smarts/.

14. http://www.adweek.com/news/technology/oreo-tries-super-bowl-tweet-strategy
    -oscars-147518.
15. https://blog.twitter.com/2013/real-time-marketing-spotlight-general-electric
    %E2%80%99s-iwanttoinvent.
16. http://www.adweek.com/adfreak/maxipad-brand-goes-blood-brilliant-reply
    -facebook-rant-144500.
17. http://www.telegraph.co.uk/foodanddrink/foodanddrinknews/9810767/Horse-meat
    -scandal-Tesco-apologises-over-hay-Twitter-post.html.

Index

About the Authors

Photo taken by Steve Garfield

Ekaterina Walter

Ekaterina Walter is a social media trailblazer and an author of the *Wall Street Journal* bestseller *Think Like Zuck: The Five Business Secrets of Facebook's Improbably Brilliant CEO Mark Zuckerberg.* A recognized business and marketing thought leader, she is a sought-after international speaker and a regular contributor to leading-edge print and online publications such as *Forbes*, *Fast Company*, *Huffington Post*, and *Entrepreneur*. Walter has led strategic and marketing innovation for brands such as Intel and Accenture, and she is currently a cofounder and CMO of BRANDERATI. She has been consistently recognized by the industry and her peers for her innovative thinking, most recently receiving a 2013 Marketer of the Year honor (SoMe Awards), and for being named among 25 Women Who Rock Social Media in 2012. Walter was featured in *Forbes* and *BusinessReviewUSA*, and her opinion has been highlighted on CNBC, ABC, NBC, *Fox News*, *First Business Chicago*, *TechCrunch*, the *Wall Street Journal*, and more. She sits on the board of directors of the Word of Mouth Marketing Association (WOMMA).

Walter is based in Portland, Oregon, and she holds a master's degree in international management from the Thunderbird School of Global Management.

Twitter: @Ekaterina.
Blog: www.ekaterinawalter .com.

Jessica Gioglio

Jessica Gioglio is a social media strategist and recognized thought leader who specializes in content and community engagement. Throughout her career, Gioglio has been a valuable contributor to the social media and communications teams at Dunkin' Donuts, TripAdvisor, State Street, and Comcast.

In addition to being a featured speaker at numerous social media and technology conferences, Gioglio covers social media best practices for the *Convince&Convert* blog. She also founded and runs *The SavvyBostonian*, a Boston-based lifestyle blog.

Gioglio is based in Boston, Massachusetts, and she holds a bachelor of science in marketing from Bentley University, with a minor in public relations.

Twitter: @SavvyBostonian.
Blog: www.thesavvybostonian.com.